# CIVIL WAR TRIVIA
# AND FACT BOOK

# CIVIL WAR TRIVIA AND FACT BOOK

## WEBB GARRISON

RUTLEDGE HILL PRESS
Nashville, Tennessee

Published in Nashville, Tennessee, by Rutledge Hill Press, Inc., 211 Seventh Avenue North, Nashville, Tennessee 37219. Distributed in Canada by H. B. Fenn and Company Ltd., 34 Nixon Rd., Bolton, Ontario L7E 1W2. Distributed in the United Kingdom by Verulan Publishing Ltd., 152A Park Street Lane, Park Street, St. Albans, Hertfordshire AL2 2AU.

Typography by D&T/Bailey, Nashville, Tennessee.

**Library of Congress Cataloging-in-Publication Data**

Garrison, Webb B.
    Civil War trivia and fact book/Webb Garrison
        p.      cm.
    Includes bibliographical references and index.
    ISBN 1-55853-160-2
    1. United States — History — Civil War, 1861–1865 — Miscellanea.
    2. Questions and answers.      I. Title
    F468.G37      1992
    973.7'076 — dc20                                        92-7273
                                                            CIP

Printed in the United States of America
7 8 — 98 97 96

# Contents

# Preface

What Confederate general could be identified at a distance by the ostrich plume in his hat? How many immigrants came to the North during the war years, and how many to the South? How many battles were fought in Virginia, and how many in Alabama?

*Civil War Trivia and Fact Book* answers these questions in the course of providing thousands of facts about the most colorful and most intriguing of American wars.

Many works were consulted in preparing this volume. Among them are *The Civil War Dictionary* by Mark Mayo Boatner III; *The Civil War Day by Day* by John S. Bowman; *The Army of the Potomac* (three volumes) by Bruce Catton; *Historical Times Illustrated Encyclopedia of the Civil War* edited by Patricia L. Faust; *The Civil War* (three volumes) by Shelby Foote; *R. E. Lee* (four volumes) by Robert Johnson; *Battles and Leaders of the Civil War* (four volumes) by Clarence Buel and Robert Johnson; *The Civil War Day by Day* by E. B. and Barbara Long; *Who Was Who in the Civil War* by Stewart Sifakis; *Statistical History of the United States from Colonial Times to the Present;* and *War of the Rebellion Official Records with Official Records of the Union and Confederate Navies* (158 volumes). Other works consulted are listed in the bibliography. Answers listed are those most widely accepted from among often diverse sets of data.

Officers are usually identified by the highest rank achieved (brevet included) in the U.S. Army, U.S. Volunteers, or state militia unit. Place of birth is indicated where known.

In the introduction to my earlier work, *A Treasury of Civil War Tales,* I wrote, "This volume does not begin to exhaust the rich lode of Civil War material available." The same is true of the present volume. Hopefully, though, *Civil War Trivia and Book of Facts* will prove to be an enjoyable challenge to every student of this most unusual of wars, the ramifications of which continue to our own time.

—Webb Garrison
Lake Junaluska, North Carolina

# CIVIL WAR TRIVIA
AND FACT BOOK

# 1

# Fighting Men
# of the C.S.A.

**Q.** What guerrilla was hanged in front of U.S. Colored Troops for the reported massacre of black prisoners at Saltville?

**A.** Champ Ferguson.

———◆———

**Q.** Who was the last surviving general of the C.S.A.?

**A.** Felix H. Robertson (Texas, 1839–1928).

———◆———

**Q.** What general was reduced to the unofficial rank of colonel after having been drunk at Mill Springs, Kentucky, in 1862?

**A.** George B. Crittenden (*b*. Kentucky).

———◆———

**Q.** What future general lent travel money to U. S. Grant when Grant resigned from the U.S. Army in California?

**A.** Simon Bolivar Buckner (*b*. Kentucky).

———◆———

**Q.** Who refused to use pepper on his food, saying it gave him pains in his left leg?

**A.** Lt. Gen. Thomas J. ("Stonewall") Jackson (*b*. Virginia).

———◆———

**Q.** Weighing in at 320 pounds, more or less, who was the heaviest Confederate general?

**A.** Abraham Buford (*b*. Kentucky).

**Q.** What brigadier general, who was once governor of Virginia, suffered constantly from pleurisy?

**A.** Henry A. Wise.

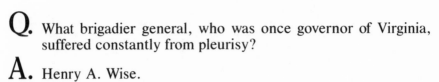

**Q.** Under the C.S.A. Furlough and Bounty Act of 1862, how much cash did a soldier receive for a three-year reenlistment?

**A.** Fifty dollars, in Confederate currency.

**Q.** What five Indian tribes furnished warriors who fought under Albert Pike?

**A.** Cherokees, Creeks, Chickasaws, Choctaws, Seminoles.

**Q.** What general was carried on the roll of a New Orleans unit as an honorary private, with the color sergeant answering "Absent on duty!" when the roster was called?

**A.** Pierre Gustave Toutant Beauregard (*b*. Louisiana).

**Q.** Who was the only general officer to fight on both sides, as a U.S. Army captain and as a C.S.A. brigadier?

**A.** Frank C. Armstrong (*b*. Indian Territory).

**Q.** What inmate of the prison at Fort Warren, Massachusetts, was promoted to the rank of major general while he was a Union prisoner of war?

**A.** John S. Marmaduke (*b*. Missouri).

**Q.** What graduate of South Carolina College, who was made a brigadier at Pensacola, saw his command virtually wiped out at Stone's River?

**A.** John K. Jackson (*b*. Georgia).

**Q.** What former Virginia Military Institute faculty member became the first combat martyr of the Confederacy?

**A.** Capt. John Marr, at Fairfax Court House, Virginia, on June 1, 1861.

---

**Q.** What Tar Heel Unionist enlisted as a private in the First North Carolina state troops, became a brigadier general, then spent twenty-three postwar years as a U.S. senator?

**A.** Matt W. Ransom (*b*. North Carolina).

---

**Q.** What Virginia colonel was commander of a prison before being placed in charge of the C.S.A. Bureau of Conscription, then fled to Europe when Lee surrendered?

**A.** John S. Preston.

---

**Q.** Who was the father of Harvard graduate Will H. ("Rooney") Lee, who became a major general after having been captured?

**A.** Gen. Robert E. Lee.

---

**Q.** Dudley M. DuBose of Georgia, a veteran of Gettysburg, the Wilderness, Petersburg, and Sayler's Creek, was captured and then held in what prison?

**A.** Fort Warren, Massachusetts.

---

**Q.** What North Carolinian cried, "Give them the cold steel!" before leading 150 men against Cemetery Ridge?

**A.** Brig. Gen. Lewis A. Armistead.

---

**Q.** What was the name of one of Barnard Bee's brothers who supervised smuggling operations from Brownsville, Texas?

**A.** Brig. Gen. Hamilton P. Bee (*b*. South Carolina).

Q. What Virginia congressman resigned to become a colonel of infantry, then resigned that commission under accusation of being a Unionist?

A. Albert Rust.

---

Q. What C.S.A. brigadier flunked out of West Point, was wounded in battle four times, and spent three years in Cuban exile?

A. Birkett Davenport Fry (*b*. Virginia).

---

Q. What Kentucky native was appointed to West Point from Louisiana, graduated eighth in the class of 1826, then later resigned from the U.S. Army to become a full general in the Confederate army?

A. Gen. Albert S. Johnston.

---

Q. A U.S. Army fort was named for what Georgia lawyer and C.S.A. brigadier general whom Lee called "Rock"?

A. Brig. Gen. Henry Lewis Benning.

---

Q. What Kentucky-born West Pointer served in the artillery, the infantry, and the cavalry?

A. Brig. Gen. Hylan Benton Lyon.

---

Q. At First Bull Run, what fellow brigadier general coined the nickname "Stonewall" for Thomas J. Jackson?

A. Bernard Bee (*b*. South Carolina).

---

Q. In what battle was Kentucky native Daniel W. Adams, a noted duelist, wounded most seriously at Shiloh, Murfreesboro, or Chickamauga?

A. Shiloh, where he lost an eye.

Q. What West Point graduate, class of 1830, was the first and only commandant of the C.S.A. Marine Corps?

A. Col. Lloyd J. Beall (*b.* Rhode Island).

———◆———

Q. Georgia native Porter Alexander, third in the West Point class of 1857, helped develop what communication system?

A. The semaphore or "wigwag" system.

---

### Dressed to Kill

Jeb Stuart of the C.S.A. kept a banjo player on his headquarters staff. As though ears filled with music were not enough to guarantee a win, he rode into battle wearing an ostrich plume in his hat and a gray coat lined with scarlet.

A colorful appearance was not limited to Rebels, however. Brig. Gen. Turner Ashby, C.S.A., wore gauntlets when he mounted his horse to meet the enemy. And, yes, a spyglass and a fox-hunting horn dangled from his saddle.

Even so, Ashby and Stuart looked drab in comparison to George Armstrong Custer, the Union's future Indian fighter. Disdaining clothing issued by the quartermaster, Custer wore a uniform tailored from blue velvet and heavily trimmed with gold.

When Custer and Stuart met at Yellow Tavern during Grant's 1864 drive upon Richmond, the warrior in velvet saw his ostrich-plumed opponent take a mortal wound.

---

Q. What Tennessean enlisted as a private, became a brigadier after Shiloh, and had six horses killed under him?

A. William B. Bate.

———◆———

Q. What was the native state of Rufus Barringer, who became a brigadier with no military experience and as a final exploit covered Lee's withdrawal from Richmond?

A. North Carolina.

[COURTESY OF FORT BENNING, GEORGIA]

*Brig. Gen. Henry L. Benning attracted little attention during the war. A Georgia attorney and state supreme court justice with no military training, he enlisted on August 15, 1861, as a colonel and gradually rose in rank. He surrendered and was paroled at Appomattox, then returned to Georgia to resume his law practice. Benning would be all but forgotten today, except for Fort Benning at Columbus, Georgia, where the U.S. Army maintains the "world's largest training program for infantrymen."*

Q. A Louisiana Creole who spoke French before he learned English and was second in the West Point class of 1838 was given what three baptismal names?

A. Pierre Gustave Toutant (Beauregard).

———◆———

Q. What Pennsylvania-born general was killed at Savage's Station, Virginia, on July 29, 1862?

A. Richard Griffith.

———◆———

Q. A fall from a horse, the result of a broken stirrup, caused the death of what Mississippi bookstore owner, a native of South Carolina, who had been captured at Vicksburg, then paroled?

A. Brig. Gen. William E. Baldwin.

**Q.** Who became an instant brigadier at Williamsburg, Virginia, because Jefferson Davis liked the way he led a charge?

**A.** George Burgwyn Anderson (*b*. North Carolina).

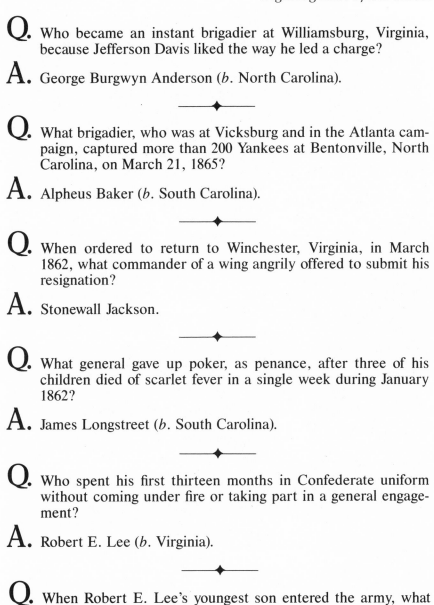

**Q.** What brigadier, who was at Vicksburg and in the Atlanta campaign, captured more than 200 Yankees at Bentonville, North Carolina, on March 21, 1865?

**A.** Alpheus Baker (*b*. South Carolina).

**Q.** When ordered to return to Winchester, Virginia, in March 1862, what commander of a wing angrily offered to submit his resignation?

**A.** Stonewall Jackson.

**Q.** What general gave up poker, as penance, after three of his children died of scarlet fever in a single week during January 1862?

**A.** James Longstreet (*b*. South Carolina).

**Q.** Who spent his first thirteen months in Confederate uniform without coming under fire or taking part in a general engagement?

**A.** Robert E. Lee (*b*. Virginia).

**Q.** When Robert E. Lee's youngest son entered the army, what was his rank and duty?

**A.** Private, cannoneer (Robert, E., Jr., age eighteen).

**Q.** What Ohio-born guerrilla leader was rewarded for his depredations by being made a C.S.A. captain?

**A.** William Clarke Quantrill.

## Yankees Who Fought under the Stars and Bars

Samuel Cooper, adjutant general of the U.S. Army since 1852, reached a turning point on March 7, 1861. On that day he decided to forget about his Hackensack, New Jersey, rearing and resigned his post to take up the same job for the Confederacy. As adjutant general, he outranked practically all native-born fighters for the Confederacy. Despite suspicions about his loyalty, he remained at his post until Appomattox.

Before First Bull Run, an estimated two dozen natives of northern states decided to cast their lot with the Confederacy; sixteen of them were graduates of West Point. Among high-ranking officers or well-known scoundrels of this group were:

Brig. Gen. Josiah Gorgas, *b*. Running Pumps, Pennsylvania.
Brig. Gen. William W. Allen, *b*. New York City.
Brig. Gen. Johnson K. Duncan, *b*. York, Pennsylvania.
Brig. Gen. William Miller, *b*. Ithaca, New York.
Brig. Gen. Edward A. Perry, *b*. Richmond, Massachusetts.
Brig. Gen. William McComb, *b*. Mercer City, Pennsylvania.
Brig. Gen. Daniel Ruggles, *b*. Barre, Massachusetts.
Lt. Gen. John C. Pemberton, *b*. Philadelphia, Pennsylvania.
Col. William C. Quantrill, *b*. Dover, Ohio.
Col. Herman Haupt, *b*. Philadelphia, Pennsylvania.
John Slidell, C.S.A. diplomatic representative in France, *b*. New York City.

**Q.** What Confederate general was a constant sufferer from migraine and dyspepsia?

**A.** Braxton Bragg (*b*. North Carolina).

◆

**Q.** What fast-moving cavalryman refused anesthesia when surgeons removed a ball lodged close to his spine?

**A.** Nathan Bedford Forrest (*b*. Tennessee).

**Q.** What general frequently strolled about camp handing out Sunday school leaflets?

**A.** Thomas Jonathan ("Stonewall") Jackson.

———◆———

**Q.** Who made comrades of deserters stand at attention while watching their friends shot by firing squads?

**A.** Gen. Braxton Bragg.

———◆———

**Q.** What nineteen-year-old sergeant took water to wounded enemies and became known as the "angel of Marye's Heights"?

**A.** Richard Rowland Kirkland (*b*. South Carolina).

———◆———

**Q.** What Boston-born brigadier general commanded Indian regiments whose warriors were charged with having scalped numerous Union soldiers?

**A.** Albert Pike.

———◆———

**Q.** Who was promoted to major general because of his capture of Plymouth, North Carolina, with its garrison of 3,000 soldiers?

**A.** Robert Frederick Hoke (*b*. North Carolina).

———◆———

**Q.** What 1854 graduate of West Point helped assault Fort Sumter, was captured at Vicksburg, and as lieutenant general commanded a southwestern department?

**A.** Stephen Dill Lee (*b*. South Carolina).

———◆———

**Q.** What major general, who graduated forty-fourth in a West Point class of fifty-two, was severely wounded in the left arm, then lost his right leg?

**A.** John Bell Hood (*b*. Kentucky).

*Maj. Henry Wirz listened as workmen erected a scaffold near the U.S. Capitol, knowing it was being built for him. Born in Switzerland, he was practicing medicine in Kentucky when the war broke out. In March 1864 his medical training caused Confederate leaders to send him to Andersonville Prison as commandant. Captured at the camp, he was tried by a military tribunal, convicted, and sentenced to death over protest of Clara Barton. Now he is listed as the only "war criminal" of the 1860s, hanged to the sound of four Federal companies chanting "Remember Andersonville."*

**Q.** A former law partner of President James K. Polk, what brigadier general was suspended from command after the debacle at Fort Donelson?

**A.** Gideon Johnson Pillow (*b.* Tennessee).

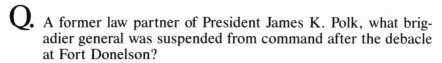

**Q.** Jedediah Hotchkiss, the self-taught map maker for Stonewall Jackson, was a native of what state?

**A.** New York.

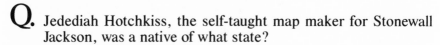

**Q.** What Massachusetts native fought at Seven Pines and White Oak Swamp, then took command of the Florida Brigade?

**A.** Brig. Gen. Edward Aylesworth Perry.

---

**Q.** Who took over the Orphan Brigade at Chickamauga, fought in the Atlanta campaign, and did not surrender until May 6, 1865?

**A.** Brig. Gen. Joseph Horace Lewis (*b.* Kentucky).

---

**Q.** What former medical professor and organizer of the ambulance corps and reserve hospitals of the C.S.A. amputated Stonewall Jackson's arm?

**A.** Hunter Holmes McGuire (*b.* Virginia).

---

**Q.** What Maryland native, once adjutant general to Sterling Price, was first buried in the garden behind his Iuka, Mississippi, headquarters?

**A.** Brig. Gen. Lewis Henry Little.

---

**Q.** Removed from command after losing his left arm and left leg, what brigadier was later governor of Louisiana for eight years?

**A.** Francis Redding Tillou Nicholls (*b.* Louisiana).

Q. What son of a minister who became a general handled Stonewall Jackson's paper work and dressed him for burial?

A. Alexander Swift Pendleton (*b*. Virginia).

———◆———

Q. What major general, a nephew of Robert E. Lee, later served as major general in the U.S. Army during the Spanish-American War?

A. Fitzhugh Lee (*b*. Virginia).

———◆———

Q. What New Jersey native was the highest ranking Confederate general, whose name was first on the first confirmation list of full generals?

A. Samuel Cooper.

———◆———

Q. What West Pointer, who was conspicuous in the Red River campaign, accepted parole in May or June 1865, then fled to France?

A. Brig. Gen. James Patrick Major (*b*. Missouri).

———◆———

Q. What brigadier general was nicknamed "Prince John" because of his grandiose behavior and was the subject of a popular song calling him "the hero for the times"?

A. John Bankhead Magruder (*b*. Virginia).

———◆———

Q. What Virginia-born artillerist named four of his cannons Matthew, Mark, Luke, and John?

A. Brig. Gen. William Nelson Pendleton, an ordained Episcopal rector.

———◆———

Q. First in his West Point class of 1854 and scion of a famous strategist, what Virginian spent most of the war as an aide to Jefferson Davis?

A. Brig. Gen. George Washington Custis Lee, eldest son of Robert E. Lee.

**Q.** Famous as "Defender of Vicksburg," what lieutenant general demoted himself to colonel of artillery?

**A.** John Clifford Pemberton (*b.* Pennsylvania).

---

**Q.** What lawyer who started as a second lieutenant in the Thirty-third Virginia was a brigadier for only ninety days before ill health forced his resignation?

**A.** Edwin Gray Lee (*b.* Virginia).

---

**Q.** Who lost Island No. 10 on the Mississippi River but became Joseph E. Johnston's chief of staff before being relieved at his own request?

**A.** William Whann Mackall (*b.* Maryland).

---

**Q.** Who claimed that his promotion to brigadier was delayed three years because of his influential family's enemies?

**A.** Arthur Middleton Manigault (*b.* Charleston, South Carolina).

---

**Q.** Who called duty "the most sublime word in the English language," disliked secession and slavery, but fought like a tiger against overwhelming odds?

**A.** Gen. Robert E. Lee.

---

**Q.** What cavalryman's raids terrorized Tennessee and Kentucky before his 1863 foray of twenty-four days into Indiana and Ohio?

**A.** Brig. Gen. John Hunt Morgan (*b.* Alabama).

---

**Q.** What brigadier general in the Confederate Provisional Army had a brother with the same rank serving in the U.S. Volunteers?

**A.** James McQueen McIntosh (*b.* Florida).

Q. What cavalry captain, who was dismissed from the U.S. Army after he resigned his commission, became a major general in the Confederate Army after Corinth, Mississippi?

A. Dabney Herndon Maury (*b.* Virginia).

———◆———

Q. After the war, what quartermaster general became president of the American Bar Association and U.S. minister to Austria?

A. Alexander Robert Lawton (*b.* South Carolina).

---

### Stonewall's Secret of Success

To an intimate, Stonewall Jackson once confessed the secret of his battlefield success: "Mystery. Mystery is the secret of success."

More than once, he sent large bodies of troops forward without revealing their destinations. When a unit reached a crossroads, its leader would be told what route to take. At each successive crossroads, he would be given another message. After following the final set of directions, the unit would arrive at its objective.

Mysterious movements were not limited to troops, however. Many of his aides said they often saw him raise his right arm and hold it aloft for many minutes. He never explained whether he did so to engage in silent prayer or to cause blood to flow downward and "establish equilibrium," which he considered essential to good health.

---

Q. When captured, what physician who had been medical director for Lee and for Early was quickly released because he never had retained captured Union surgeons?

A. Hunter Holmes McGuire (*b.* Virginia).

———◆———

Q. What brigadier of many names led his troops to victory at Pleasant Grove, Louisiana, before falling with 690 of his men?

A. Jean Jacques Alfred Alexander Mouton (*b.* Louisiana).

**Q.** With only 60,000 men at his command, how many casualties did Robert E. Lee inflict on the 120,000-man Union army while defending Richmond?

**A.** Fifty thousand.

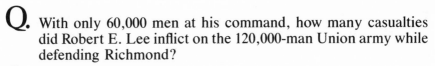

**Q.** What lieutenant general, who fought in the Atlanta, Franklin, and Nashville campaigns, became a promoter of women's rights after the war?

**A.** Stephen Dill Lee (*b.* South Carolina).

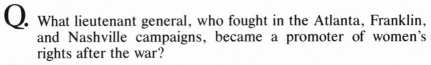

**Q.** What brigadier general's running feud with generals Micah Jenkins and James Longstreet led to his temporary resignation?

**A.** Evander McIvor Law (*b.* South Carolina; resigned December 19, 1863).

**Q.** After the war, when Robert E. Lee became president of Washington College, what was his annual salary?

**A.** $1,500.

**Q.** What member of the U.S. garrison defending Fort Sumter later fought for the C.S.A.?

**A.** Richard Kidder Meade (*b.* Virginia).

**Q.** What former U.S. secretary of war was relieved of his command by another former secretary of war?

**A.** Brig. Gen. John B. Floyd, by Jefferson Davis.

**Q.** In what battle did some Confederate general officers and many men wear uniforms of the U.S. Army?

**A.** First Bull Run (Generals Johnston, Beauregard, Longstreet).

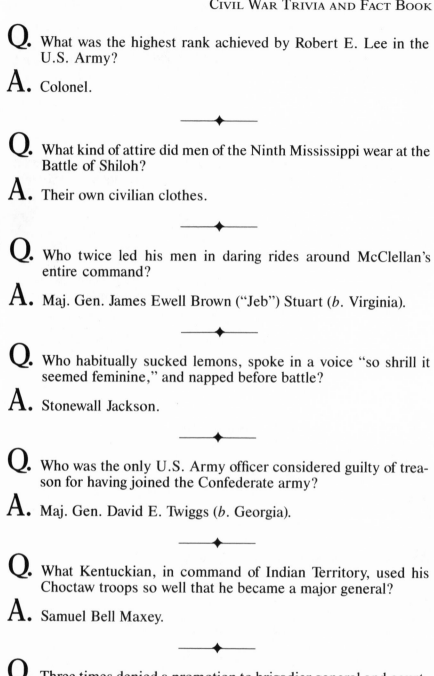

**Q.** What was the highest rank achieved by Robert E. Lee in the U.S. Army?

**A.** Colonel.

---

**Q.** What kind of attire did men of the Ninth Mississippi wear at the Battle of Shiloh?

**A.** Their own civilian clothes.

---

**Q.** Who twice led his men in daring rides around McClellan's entire command?

**A.** Maj. Gen. James Ewell Brown ("Jeb") Stuart (*b.* Virginia).

---

**Q.** Who habitually sucked lemons, spoke in a voice "so shrill it seemed feminine," and napped before battle?

**A.** Stonewall Jackson.

---

**Q.** Who was the only U.S. Army officer considered guilty of treason for having joined the Confederate army?

**A.** Maj. Gen. David E. Twiggs (*b.* Georgia).

---

**Q.** What Kentuckian, in command of Indian Territory, used his Choctaw troops so well that he became a major general?

**A.** Samuel Bell Maxey.

---

**Q.** Three times denied a promotion to brigadier general and court-martialed by Gen. Thomas L. Rosser, who led the Second Virginia to the Carolinas after Appomattox, hoping to continue the fight there?

**A.** Thomas Taylor Munford (*b.* Virginia).

*Bishop-general Leonidas Polk graduated from West Point in 1827, then took off his uniform to become an Episcopal priest. His long-time friend Jefferson Davis persuaded him to put on Confederate gray on June 25, 1861, starting as a major general. He retained his office as Episcopal bishop of Louisiana and was the only high-ranking member of the clergy to die instantly from an artillery shell. He was hit and killed at Pine Mountain, Georgia, on June 24, 1864.*

Q. Who led the left-flank charge against Cemetery Ridge, lost 50 percent of his men, and was last to leave the field?

A. Brig. Gen. James Henry Lane (*b.* Virginia).

Q. What entire unit from Charleston, South Carolina, entered C.S.A. service wearing blue Federal uniforms?

A. The Flying Artillery.

Q. What close friend of Jefferson Davis was simultaneously a naval lieutenant and a colonel of cavalry?

A. John Taylor Wood (*b.* Iowa Territory).

Q. The troops of what major general constituted the only Confederate force that actively opposed Sherman's March to the Sea?

A. Joseph Wheeler (*b.* Georgia).

**Q.** What West Point graduate of the class of 1827 baptized Gen. John Bell Hood during the Atlanta campaign?

**A.** The bishop-general, Leonidas Polk (*b*. North Carolina).

------◆------

**Q.** What physician was the only prison commandant to be executed for "war crimes"?

**A.** Heinrich Hartmann Wirz, head of Andersonville (*b*. Switzerland).

------◆------

**Q.** On January 19, 1862, what nearsighted former congressman and newspaper editor was killed at Mill Springs, Kentucky, his first and only battle?

**A.** Brig. Gen. Felix Kirk Zollicoffer (*b*. Tennessee).

------◆------

**Q.** What soldier of fortune, who had fought with Garibaldi for the unification of Italy in 1860, led a company of former convicts from New Orleans that was called the "Tiger Rifles"?

**A.** Chatham Roberdeau Wheat (*b*. Virginia).

------◆------

**Q.** What major general, promoted after only four months as a brigadier, ordered the burning of Norfolk's navy yard, which destroyed the CSS *Virginia?*

**A.** Benjamin Huger (*b*. South Carolina).

------◆------

**Q.** What graduate of the West Point class of 1831 was made commissary general by Jefferson Davis?

**A.** Lucius Bellinger Northrop (*b*. South Carolina).

------◆------

**Q.** What teacher-lawyer, wounded during Pickett's charge, was a postwar congressman, senator, and the only southern commissioner to decide the disputed presidential election of 1876?

**A.** Brig. Gen. Eppa Hunton (*b*. Virginia).

## Highly Symbolic Black

At the outbreak of war, Joseph O. Shelby of Lexington, Kentucky, declined an offer of a captain's commission in the Union army. Instead, he chose to fight for states' rights and for preservation of laws that kept blacks in slavery. Wearing a conspicuous black plume in his hat, the Kentucky cavalryman fought in every major campaign in Missouri and Arkansas.

---◆---

Tennessee-born Ben McCulloch, who went to Texas very early and was a leader of the republic, commissioned a tailor to make for him a special "fighting suit"—not a uniform—of black velvet. He was a leader of southern fighting men who favored a Black Flag policy under which all captured Yankees who had fought alongside blacks would be shot on the spot.

**Q.** What full general was disgruntled because he thought his U.S. Army rank should have transferred to the Confederate army, thus making him the senior general instead of the fourth in seniority?

**A.** Joseph Eggleston Johnston (*b.* Virginia).

---◆---

**Q.** What former Indian fighter who, when pursued by Federal forces in September 1862, lost only his trademark, a plumed hat?

**A.** Maj. Gen. James Ewell Brown ("Jeb") Stuart.

---◆---

**Q.** What twenty-eight-year-old major improved artillery tactics so that his "flying battery" appeared to be double in size?

**A.** Maj. John Pelham (*b.* Alabama).

Q. What West Pointer, class of 1838, took over Stonewall Jackson's division after Jackson's death at Chancellorsville?

A. Maj. Gen. Edward Johnson (*b*. Virginia).

———◆———

Q. Who was captured first at Williamsburg, Virginia, in May 1862, a second time at Gettysburg in July 1863, and was arrested a third time by Federal troops the night of Lincoln's assassination, although the war was then over?

A. Brig. Gen. William Henry Fitzhugh Payne (*b*. Virginia).

———◆———

Q. Possibly suffering psychological disorders, what lieutenant general frequently reported himself ill during times of crisis, thus avoiding responsibility?

A. Ambrose Powell Hill (*b*. Virginia).

———◆———

Q. What friend and former comrade in arms of U. S. Grant was forced to accept his terms of unconditional surrender at Fort Donelson?

A. Maj. Gen. Simon Bolivar Buckner (*b*. Kentucky).

———◆———

Q. Who was Robert E. Lee's military secretary?

A. Col. Armistead Lindsay Long (*b*. Virginia).

———◆———

Q. What fellow townsman whom Stonewall Jackson appointed to his staff and assigned to command the Stonewall Brigade was killed at Chancellorsville in May 1863?

A. Brig. Gen. Elisha Franklin Paxton (*b*. Virginia).

———◆———

Q. What Rhode Island native, the son of an artillery captain from Virginia, refused to surrender with Lee in Virginia?

A. Maj. Gen. Lunsford Lindsay Lomax.

*Kentucky-born John B. Hood lost a leg at Chickamauga and spent weeks recuperating in Richmond. He was seen most often in poker dens, where he soon made a reputation for reckless play and high stakes. One of his rueful opponents insisted he saw Hood win after betting $2,000 on a hand without a single pair.*

*Jefferson Davis was no poker player, but he invited the gallant young general to drawing rooms of the Confederate White House and became extremely fond of him. When Joseph E. Johnston angered the C.S.A. president by fighting a long rear-guard action against Sherman's army, he was replaced by the younger man noted for his reckless daring.*

*But the hills around Atlanta were no poker table; Hood switched the game plan and repeatedly took the offensive. As a result, Davis's protégé lost Atlanta. Some believe that when Atlanta was lost, total defeat of the C.S.A. became only a matter of time.*

Q. Not having heard of Lee's surrender, who scored a victory in the war's last land battle on May 12–13, 1865, at Palmito Ranch, Texas?

A. Texas Ranger John S. ("Rest in Peace") Ford.

◆

Q. Since Kentucky was not in the Confederacy and its forces were driven from it in 1862, what nickname was given to the famed First Kentucky Brigade?

A. The Orphan Brigade.

◆

Q. What 300-pound spiritualist from Kentucky fought in West Virginia for six months, then resigned?

A. Brig. Gen. Marshall Humphrey (*b.* Kentucky).

◆

Q. What major general caused Stonewall Jackson to submit his resignation, but the feud was mitigated for the good of the Confederacy?

A. William Wing Loring (*b.* North Carolina).

◆

Q. What brigadier general, a Baptist minister, participated in a religious revival in 1864, baptizing more than fifty soldiers?

A. Mark Perrin Lowrey (*b.* Tennessee).

◆

Q. Who surrendered Louisiana's Federal supply depot to state troops and then became the C.S.A. quartermaster general?

A. Brig. Gen. Abraham Charles Myers (*b.* South Carolina).

◆

Q. Whose activities as a Partisan Ranger were so successful that General Grant ordered that he be hanged without trial if captured?

A. John Singleton Mosby (*b.* Virginia).

**Q.** What major general, later relieved of command, was the subject of a scurrilous ballad composed by his troops depicting his loss of New Orleans and his red nose, the result of heavy drinking?

**A.** Mansfield Lovell (*b.* District of Columbia).

---

**Q.** What native of North Carolina resigned his command after his overwhelming defeat at Missionary Ridge?

**A.** Gen. Braxton Bragg.

---

**Q.** Following the death of Brig. Gen. Micah Jenkins, who led Jenkins's brigade so well that he became "Old Reliable"?

**A.** Brig. Gen. John Bratton (*b.* South Carolina).

---

### Score Keeper

Brig. Gen. John D. Kennedy, C.S.A., was hit by a minié ball at First Bull Run. Having duly recorded the injury in his journal, he decided to keep score. Severely wounded at Gettysburg, he was sent South to recover. Fighting under Johnston in the Carolina campaign, he received his third, fourth, fifth, sixth, seventh, and eighth wounds. In addition, he wrote, "On fifteen separate occasions I was hit by spent balls."

---

**Q.** What subordinate of Nathan Bedford Forrest, formerly an infantryman, was called "Little 'Un" by his men?

**A.** Col. James Ronald Chalmers (*b.* Virginia).

---

**Q.** What later chief of staff to Gen. Robert E. Lee saved the life of the wounded Jefferson Davis by carrying him to safety during the battle of Buena Vista in the Mexican War?

**A.** Robert Hall Chilton (*b.* Virginia).

Q. What C.S.A. congressman formed a "mixed legion" of 600 infantry, 300 cavalry, and 100 artillerists?

A. Thomas R. R. Cobb (*b*. Georgia).

---

Q. Who lost several teeth to a bullet in Richmond, Kentucky, but won a promotion for action there?

A. Brig. Gen. Patrick Ronayne Cleburne (*b*. Ireland).

---

Q. What brigadier general led 200 men against 2,000 near Blue Mountain, Alabama, on July 14, 1864?

A. James Holt Clanton (*b*. Georgia).

---

Q. Because of dispatches to London newspapers, what cavalryman had an international reputation by the end of 1862?

A. Brig. Gen. J. E. B. ("Jeb") Stuart (*b*. Virginia).

---

Q. Who was the only man on either side, Confederate or Union, who started in the war as a private and ended as a lieutenant general?

A. Nathan Bedford Forrest (*b*. Tennessee).

---

Q. At what battle did General Lee's famous horse Traveller become uncharacteristically frightened by a bursting shell, rearing just in time for a cannonball to pass harmlessly under his girth?

A. Spotsylvania.

# 2

# Fighting Men of the U.S.A.

**Q.** What friend of Abraham Lincoln formed Chicago's Zouave Cadets and the New York Fire Zouaves?

**A.** Col. Elmer Ellsworth (*b*. New York).

———◆———

**Q.** What was unusual about the appearance of zouave units?

**A.** Colorful, exotic uniforms modeled on French Algerian tribal garb which the troops wore although they made good targets.

———◆———

**Q.** How many defenders of Fort Sumter later became major generals?

**A.** Six: Anderson, Crawford, Davis, Doubleday, Foster, and Seymour.

———◆———

**Q.** How many regiments wore Federal blue uniforms at First Bull Run (First Manassas)?

**A.** None, as such uniforms had not yet been issued.

———◆———

**Q.** When did U. S. Grant quit trimming his beard and for a short time permit it to grow full length?

**A.** When he was made colonel of the Twenty-first Illinois in June 1861.

**Q.** What brigadier general in the Corps of Engineers supervised the completion of the Washington Monument after the war?

**A.** Horatio Gouverneur Wright.

---

**Q.** Who had as subordinates the Comte de Paris, the Duc de Chartres, and the Prince de Joinville?

**A.** Maj. Gen. George B. McClellan (*b.* Pennsylvania).

---

**Q.** What prisoners at Castle Pinckney in Charleston wore blue trousers and jackets, red flannel shirts, and red fez caps?

**A.** Fire Zouaves of New York, the Eleventh New York.

---

**Q.** Who was the last surviving full-rank Civil War general?

**A.** Adelbert Ames (*b.* Maine, 1835; *d.* Florida, 1933).

---

**Q.** When the Civil War began, what future general tried to answer the call for volunteers but was rejected?

**A.** U. S. Grant.

---

**Q.** What Ohio native entered the army in the Civil War as a lieutenant colonel and died as commander in chief?

**A.** James A. Garfield, assassinated while serving as twentieth president of the United States.

---

**Q.** What grandson of a president of the United States entered service as a second lieutenant of the Seventieth Regiment of Indiana Volunteers and rose to the rank of brigadier general by the end of the war?

**A.** Benjamin Harrison, later twenty-third president of the United States.

Criminal attorney Benjamin F. Butler, a prominent Democrat, was one of Abraham Lincoln's early choices as "a political general." As the military commander of New Orleans, he assumed dictatorial powers and ordered William Mumford hanged for tearing down a U.S. flag—action for which he was widely condemned. A bit later he became known as Beast Butler when he ordered that any New Orleans woman who showed contempt for a Federal soldier should be treated as a woman of the street. Despite significant military victories, his most important contribution to the Union war effort was his decision to treat runaway slaves as contraband of war. This meant that, despite the fact that commander in chief Lincoln supported the Fugitive Slave Law, Butler refused to obey it.

**Q.** What lawyer went to war as major of the Twenty-third Ohio, attained the rank of brevet major general, and later said that those years were "the best years" of his life?

**A.** Rutherford B. Hayes, nineteenth president of the United States.

———◆———

**Q.** What future major general entered West Point at age fifteen and in 1846 graduated second in his class?

**A.** George B. McClellan (*b.* Pennsylvania).

———◆———

**Q.** While coats of most officers of junior grade had fourteen buttons arranged in seven rows, what officer's coat had sixteen?

**A.** A brigadier general's.

**Q.** Service at Mobile won the third star for what Hoosier attorney with no military experience before the war?

**A.** James Clifford Veatch.

———◆———

**Q.** What senior brigadier of the army in 1861, when McClellan was promoted over his head, got Fort Monroe exempted from McClellan's jurisdiction so he would not have to take orders from him?

**A.** John Ellis Wool (*b.* New York).

———◆———

**Q.** What captain at Fort Sumter, who has sometimes been credited with firing the first shot of the war there, has been erroneously credited with inventing a popular sport?

**A.** Abner Doubleday, once regarded as the father of baseball (*b.* New York).

———◆———

**Q.** What naval officer had a chamber pot emptied upon his head in occupied New Orleans?

**A.** Capt. David G. Farragut (*b.* Tennessee).

———◆———

**Q.** In New Orleans, who issued the infamous Woman's Order, whereby any female would be treated as a practicing prostitute if it were deemed she showed disrespect by word or gesture to any Union officer or enlisted man?

**A.** Maj. Gen. Benjamin F. Butler (*b.* New Hampshire).

———◆———

**Q.** Because of his treatment of civilians, by what name was Maj. Gen. Benjamin F. Butler, military governor of Louisiana, known for the rest of his career?

**A.** "Beast."

———◆———

**Q.** At what battle did at least thirty members of militia units take to the field for each man in the U.S. Army?

**A.** First Bull Run.

## Natives of "Slave States" Who Fought for the North

Virginia-born George H. Thomas was forty-five years old when the war began and a professional soldier in the U.S. Army. His relatives took it for granted that he would resign to enter Confederate service. When he failed to do so, they ostracized him; many Union leaders suspected him of planning treachery. Still, the man from Southampton City rose to the rank of major general. After becoming famous as the Rock of Chickamauga, he was made second in command to Sherman for the Atlanta Campaign.

When fighting was imminent, nearly 300 natives of southern and border states were U.S. Army officers. Thomas was just one of an estimated eighty of them who continued to serve the Union. A number of men born in slave states gave distinguished service to the Union; others were more colorful than distinguished. Here are just a few of them:

Quartermaster Gen. Montgomery M. Meigs, *b*. Augusta, Georgia.

Vice Adm. David G. Farragut, *b*. Campbell's Station, Tennessee.

Brig. Gen. Benjamin M. Prentiss, *b*. Belleville, Virginia.

Maj. Gen. David B. Birney, *b*. Huntsville, Alabama.

Capt. Percival Drayton, *b*. Charleston, South Carolina.

Brig. Gen. Robert Anderson, *b*. near Louisville, Kentucky

Maj. Gen. Alexander Brydie, *b*. Richmond, Virginia.

Maj. Gen. Alvan Cullen, *b*. Gainesboro, Tennessee.

Brig. Gen. John B. McIntosh, *b*. Fort Brooke, Florida.

Cmdr. William D. Porter, *b*. New Orleans, Louisiana.

Brig. Gen. Lorenzo Thomas, *b*. New Castle, Delaware.

Cmdr. John A. Winslow, *b*. Wilmington, North Carolina.

Brig. Gen. Jesse L. Reno, *b*. Wheeling, [now West] Virginia.

"Parson" William G. ("Parson") Brownlow, *b*. Wythe City, Virginia.

Col. Louis Marshall of Virginia—one of Gen. John Pope's couriers—once took a vital message to the enemy commander, who was also his uncle, Robert E. Lee.

## Money Matters

Far and away the most popular song of Union troops came from the pen of a woman. Julia Ward Howe was inspired to write the "Battle Hymn of the Republic" during a visit to wartime Washington. When editors of the *Atlantic Monthly* graciously agreed to print her song, they paid the author five dollars.

———◆———

Reluctant to use black soldiers but aware that they would boost the strength of Union armies, Abraham Lincoln signed a congressional bill that authorized their enlistment. Under terms of the measure, a black fighting man received a trifle more than half the pay given to a white comrade in arms.

Indignant members of the Massachusetts Fifty-fourth and Fifty-fifth protested, but got no results. These militant blacks remained in uniform but refused pay for eighteen months, until a presidential order brought equality between blacks and whites at the paymaster's tent.

Q. After having volunteered for ninety days of federal service, how long were many militia members required to stay in uniform?

A. Three years.

———◆———

Q. What Illinois native, a brigadier general at twenty-nine, was the only Union general to outmaneuver and outmarch Nathan Bedford Forrest, in a raid to Selma, Alabama, March 22–April 2, 1865?

A. James Harrison Wilson.

———◆———

Q. After failing to follow instructions at the battle of Franklin in November 1864, what brigadier general requested leave from duty "because of my wife's health"?

A. George Day Wagner (*b*. Ohio).

**Q.** What eleven-month prisoner of war, who was promoted on August 19, 1862, the day of his release, had to wait eight years for the Medal of Honor?

**A.** Maj. Gen. Orlando Bolivar Wilcox (*b.* Ohio).

---

**Q.** What brigadier, promoted after Antietam, faced a court of inquiry in the aftermath of Five Forks?

**A.** Maj. Gen. Gouverneur Kemble Warren (*b.* New York).

---

**Q.** Who formed an African Brigade from former North Carolina slaves and made them part of the force that occupied Richmond?

**A.** Brig. Gen. Edward Augustus Wild (*b.* Massachusetts).

---

**Q.** What Maine-born major general served in postwar years as governor of Wisconsin, as a U.S. congressman, and as founder of the company that became General Mills Corporation?

**A.** Cadwallader Colden Washburn.

---

**Q.** A notable achievement of Gov. John Albion Andrew of Massachusetts was to raise what famous black regiment?

**A.** The Fifty-fourth Massachusetts.

---

**Q.** What brigadier general, who was applauded by Abraham Lincoln for his protection of prisoners from a mob of civilians after First Bull Run, won the Medal of Honor for action at Jonesboro, Georgia?

**A.** Absalom Baird (*b.* Pennsylvania).

---

**Q.** Who accepted the surrender of the arms of the Army of Northern Virginia?

**A.** Maj. Gen. Joseph Jackson Bartlett (*b.* New York).

*When the upcoming election of 1864 persuaded Abraham Lincoln to turn the war over to a professional, he chose Ulysses S. Grant and put him in charge with the rank of lieutenant general. Many of Grant's aides, who "went to Hell and back" for him, reported that he had only one passionate love: horses. While a cadet at West Point, he executed better than passable drawings of horses. To some of those who worked most closely with him, it seemed strange that Grant was so shy that he went to great lengths to prevent a comrade in arms from seeing him naked.*

**Q.** What honorary brigadier general from New York organized a corps of skilled marksmen armed with fine rifles that bears his name?

**A.** Hiram G. Berdan, Berdan's Sharpshooters.

---

**Q.** How many men donned blue uniforms after having been hired as substitutes for those who did not want to fight?

**A.** At least 116,000.

---

**Q.** What top amateur rifle shot of the nation joined the army as a colonel in 1861 and received only honorary promotions thereafter?

**A.** Hiram G. Berdan (*b.* New York).

---

**Q.** Of the 292,000 men drafted in August 1863, how many met their obligation by paying the $300 commutation fee?

**A.** About 52,000, or 18 percent.

---

**Q.** What was unusual about the 430 casualties from the Tenth Corps at Chaffin's Farm, led by Maj. Gen. David Birney's brother William?

**A.** Except for officers, all were black.

---

**Q.** As an unenrolled drummer, nine-year-old Johnny Clem of Ohio received how much pay?

**A.** Thirteen dollars per month, which was soldier's pay but was contributed by officers and men of the Twenty-second Michigan.

---

**Q.** What native of Illinois claimed to have killed fifty Confederates with fifty shots from his special rifle?

**A.** James Butler ("Wild Bill") Hickok.

**Q.** Upon learning that he would face Lee instead of Johnston, who described Lee as "timid and irresolute"?

**A.** George B. McClellan.

———◆———

**Q.** Eager to display his strength, what general habitually showed off by lifting his wife to a seat on the mantelpiece?

**A.** Maj. Gen. Don Carlos Buell (*b*. Ohio).

———◆———

**Q.** What major general permitted Col. John B. Turchin, formerly Ivan Vasilevich Turchininov of the Imperial Russian Army, to command a brigade?

**A.** Ormsby MacKnight Mitchel (*b*. Kentucky).

———◆———

**Q.** After losing his plumed hat, Jeb Stuart offered to swap it for whose captured dress coat and hat?

**A.** Maj. Gen. John Pope (*b*. Kentucky).

———◆———

**Q.** What native of Ohio invented a special hat of canvas and bamboo to shield his head from Virginia heat?

**A.** Maj. Gen. Irvin McDowell.

———◆———

**Q.** What redheaded general, named for an Indian chieftain, was known to relatives and intimates as "Cump"?

**A.** William Tecumseh Sherman (*b*. Ohio).

———◆———

**Q.** What leader, more at home with horses than with men, never let subordinates see him naked?

**A.** U. S. Grant.

———◆———

**Q.** What unusual piece of equipment did General McClellan carry with him into the field?

**A.** A portable printing press, used to produce notices.

**Q.** What general officer would not touch alcohol but ate so heartily that he suffered from chronic indigestion?

**A.** Maj. Gen. Irvin McDowell (*b*. Ohio).

———◆———

**Q.** Why did some members of Federal units refuse to fight at First Bull Run?

**A.** Their ninety-day enlistments expired that day.

———◆———

**Q.** What aging hero who could not mount into a saddle feasted on terrapin at every opportunity?

**A.** Gen. of the Army Winfield Scott (*b*. Virginia).

———◆———

**Q.** What former ambassador to Russia, who became a major general without a command, claimed much credit for the Emancipation Proclamation?

**A.** Cassius Marcellus Clay (*b*. Kentucky).

———◆———

**Q.** What refugee, the leader of a division of Germans, was relieved of command after defeat at Cross Keys by Stonewall Jackson?

**A.** Brig. Gen. Louis Blenker (*b*. Germany).

———◆———

**Q.** What was the name of the "Fighting Parson," former presiding elder of the Rocky Mountain Methodist District, who butchered between 400 and 600 Cheyenne Indian villagers in the Sand Creek massacre?

**A.** Col. John Milton Chivington (*b*. Ohio).

———◆———

**Q.** What brevet major general survived the Civil War but achieved greater fame as a lieutenant colonel who died in 1876 in the battle of Little Big Horn?

**A.** George Armstrong Custer (*b*. Ohio).

**Q.** A nationally acclaimed astronomer who was influential in establishing the Naval Observatory, what major general died of yellow fever in 1862 while commanding the Department of the South?

**A.** Ormsby M. Mitchell (*b.* Kentucky).

———◆———

**Q.** What overly cautious field general was removed from command because he failed to pursue Braxton Bragg after defeating him at Perryville, Kentucky?

**A.** Don Carlos Buell (*b.* Ohio).

———◆———

**Q.** A "grateful" nation awarded the Medal of Honor thirty years after what officer led a bayonet charge at Little Round Top that broke the last Confederate onslaught at Gettysburg?

**A.** Col. Joshua Lawrence Chamberlain (*b.* Maine).

———◆———

**Q.** Removed from combat duty after blunders at Shiloh, what inept soldier became a famous novelist?

**A.** Maj. Gen. Lew Wallace, author of *Ben Hur* (*b.* Indiana).

———◆———

**Q.** What general who pursued a lifetime career in army administration was chief of staff to George H. Thomas from Missionary Ridge to Nashville?

**A.** William Denison Whipple (*b.* New York).

———◆———

**Q.** What army colonel, the grandson of a fur trader, brought with him to his Washington post his valet, chef, and steward?

**A.** John Jacob Astor III (*b.* New York).

———◆———

**Q.** Why did Edward Dickinson Baker refuse to accept appointment as a general from his old friend Abraham Lincoln?

**A.** Acceptance of a generalship would have required him to give up his seat in the U.S. Senate (from Oregon).

[LESLIE'S ILLUSTRATED WEEKLY]

*Kentucky-born Robert Anderson is widely believed to have been the officer who swore Abraham Lincoln into service for the Black Hawk War. A major by the time the situation became tense in Charleston, South Carolina, he was sent to take command of Fort Moultrie. Strong southern ties may have dictated the choice. Anderson was not considered a troublemaker, but he fooled his superiors. Without orders from Washington, he transferred to Fort Sumter because it was much stronger than Moultrie. Stubbornly refusing to yield the site, his role in launching the war was central. When ill health forced his retirement, Abraham Lincoln rewarded his loyalty by making him a major general.*

**Q.** What did General McClellan call General in Chief Winfield Scott's famous Anaconda Plan, designed early in the war to envelope and strangle the South?

**A.** "Scott's boa-constrictor plan."

———◆———

**Q.** What common disease briefly incapacitated Lincoln's general in chief, Henry W. Halleck?

**A.** Measles.

———◆———

**Q.** Late in 1861, what illness put McClellan on the sick list for three weeks?

**A.** Typhoid fever.

———◆———

**Q.** Although he was known to fellow cadets at West Point as Uncle Sam, with what name was Gen. U. S. Grant christened?

**A.** Hiram Ulysses.

———◆———

**Q.** What former fur trapper, mountain man, and scout was breveted brigadier general for his valor at Glorieta Pass and in the Indian campaigns?

**A.** Christopher ("Kit") Carson (*b*. Kentucky).

———◆———

**Q.** Whom did General in Chief Halleck authorize General McClellan to arrest after Fort Donelson because he was reputed to have "resumed his bad prewar habits"?

**A.** U. S. Grant.

———◆———

**Q.** Promoted at age thirty-four to major general after Fort Donelson, who was at that time the youngest of his rank in the entire army?

**A.** Maj. Gen. Lewis Wallace (*b*. Indiana).

Q. What was the highest rank William Tecumseh Sherman reached?

A. General of the army, with the rank of full general (succeeding U. S. Grant when he became president).

———◆———

Q. What West Pointer, twenty-first of thirty-nine in the class of 1843, was a better than passable artist, specializing in horses?

A. U. S. Grant.

———◆———

Q. At the 1860 Democratic convention in Charleston, South Carolina, what future general voted fifty-seven times to nominate Jefferson Davis for president of the United States?

A. Benjamin F. Butler (*b*. New Hampshire).

———◆———

Q. What unit led the vanguard in the attack upon Fort Wagner, South Carolina?

A. The Fifty-fourth Massachusetts, led by Col. Robert Gould Shaw.

———◆———

Q. What former Indian fighter was the highest ranking officer captured during the war?

A. Maj. Gen. George Crook (*b*. Ohio).

———◆———

Q. What body of stalwarts was mustered into defense of Washington when Confederate attack seemed imminent?

A. Government clerks.

———◆———

Q. When riding his horse, what general had to hold the reins between his teeth because his left arm was missing?

A. Maj. Gen. Philip Kearny (*b*. New York).

Q. What inept leader on whom Lincoln was forced to depend for a while was characterized as "little more than a first-rate clerk"?

A. Gen. in Chief Henry Wager Halleck (*b*. New York).

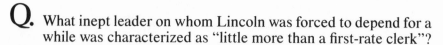

Q. Of whom was Salmon P. Chase speaking when he said that giving the Army of the Potomac to him "is equivalent to giving Washington to the Rebels"?

A. Maj. Gen. George Brinton McClellan (*b*. Pennsylvania).

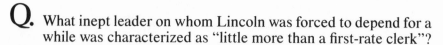

Q. When he was removed from command of the Army of Virginia, where was Maj. Gen. John Pope sent to fight?

A. Minnesota, against the Sioux Indians.

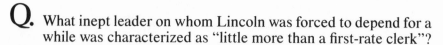

Q. To whom did General Grant give command of the prolonged siege operations at Petersburg, Virginia, in 1864?

A. Brig. Gen. Henry Jackson Hunt (*b*. Michigan).

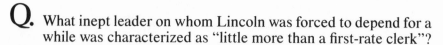

Q. On September 13, 1862, what enlisted man found Robert E. Lee's famous Lost Order, which had been carelessly dropped by a Confederate staff officer?

A. Pvt. Barton W. Mitchell of Company E, Twenty-seventh Indiana.

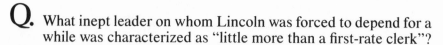

Q. What member of the West Point class of 1822 would take off his hat to reveal his long white hair when riding among his men?

A. Brig. Gen. Joseph King Fenno Mansfield (*b*. Connecticut).

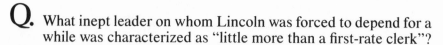

Q. While Maj. Robert Anderson surrendered Fort Sumter on April 14, 1861, who raised the Stars and Stripes there exactly four years later?

A. The same Robert Anderson, retired as a brigadier general because of poor health.

**Q.** Second in his West Point class of 1850, what chief engineer of the Army of the Potomac first saw the importance of the Round Tops at Gettysburg?

**A.** Maj. Gen. Gouverneur Kemble Warren (*b*. New York).

---

**Q.** What general declared fleeing black slaves "contrabands of war"?

**A.** Maj. Gen. Benjamin Franklin Butler (*b*. New Hampshire).

---

**Q.** What general, who changed a standard bugle call into "Taps" to signify lights out, was honored by burial at West Point although he had not attended it?

**A.** Brig. Gen. Daniel Butterfield (*b*. New York).

---

**Q.** What general commanded the all-black Twenty-fifth Corps from the Petersburg siege through the occupation of Richmond?

**A.** Maj. Gen. Godfrey Weitzel (*b*. Ohio).

---

**Q.** After the debacle at Second Bull Run, Maj. Gen. John Pope accused which of his fellow generals of disloyalty, disobedience, and misconduct under fire, which resulted in his being cashiered from the army?

**A.** Maj. Gen. Fitz-John Porter (*b*. New Hampshire).

---

**Q.** At Antietam (Sharpsburg), how many men did McClellan hold in reserve, thinking Lee's forces outnumbered his own?

**A.** 20,000, about one-fourth of his effective total.

---

**Q.** What major general murdered a fellow major general, William Nelson, at the Galt House hotel in Louisville, Kentucky, and was never charged or punished?

**A.** Maj. Gen. Jefferson Columbus ("Jeff") Davis (*b*. Indiana).

Q. What West Point classmate from 1842 did Earl Van Dorn of the C.S.A. face at Corinth, Mississippi?

A. Maj. Gen. William Starke Rosecrans (*b*. Ohio).

———◆———

Q. General Rosecrans, who was red-faced and "had the profile of a Roman senator," was given what nickname by his men?

A. Old Rosy.

———◆———

Q. What slavery-hating Alabama native was accused by Generals Heintzelman and Meade of disobeying orders?

A. Maj. Gen. David Bell Birney.

---

### Headed for the White House

Most of the 950 men who made up the Twenty-third Ohio, mustered into service in June 1862, swore that it was the finest unit in Federal service. At the time, no one guessed that both Maj. William McKinley and Col. Rutherford B. Hayes would occupy the White House before the turn of the century.

———◆———

Another pair of future notables fought together at Shiloh. Brig. Gen. James A. Garfield did not arrive until the second day was nearly over, so his brigade made no impact there. Fighting under the command of William T. Sherman, Maj. Gen. U. S. Grant was surprised and almost routed at Pittsburg Landing. He repulsed Confederates on the second day, weathered severe criticism, and became the nation's eighteenth president.

———◆———

Strangely, perhaps, no comparable pair of Confederates can be found. As a matter of fact, until long after the war ended, no Confederate veteran ever was in the White House except as a visitor on a special occasion.

**Q.** Who led 2,000 men of the California Column in a sweep through Arizona, New Mexico, and part of Texas?

**A.** Col. (later Brig. Gen.) James Henry Carleton (*b*. Maine).

---

**Q.** Whose name was omitted from all future newspaper stories in retaliation for his having expelled a reporter from the Army of the Potomac?

**A.** Maj. Gen. George Gordon Meade (*b*. Spain).

---

**Q.** What scientist, a pioneer in balloon flights, did President Lincoln make chief of army aeronautics at a colonel's pay?

**A.** Thaddeus Sobieski Constantine Lowe (*b*. New Hampshire).

---

**Q.** One of the few Southerners to become a Union general, what ordnance expert made great innovations in weaponry, increased rifle production tremendously, and himself invented a new heavy-artillery shell?

**A.** Alexander Brydie Dyer (*b*. Virginia).

---

**Q.** A favorite of Grant who led troops called Greyhounds, what brigadier general was transferred to New Mexico because it was thought it would help his tubercular condition?

**A.** Marcellus Monroe Crocker (*b*. Indiana).

---

**Q.** What influential leader strongly opposed awarding medals or decorations of any kind to fighting men because doing so was contrary to American egalitarian principles?

**A.** Lt. Gen. Winfield Scott (*b*. Virginia).

---

**Q.** With more than 5,000 men deserting monthly, what was the reward for returning a deserter to his unit?

**A.** Five dollars at first; raised to thirty dollars by 1865.

Q. What Bureau of Military Justice head led the government's prosecution of John Wilkes Booth?

A. Joseph Holt (*b*. Kentucky).

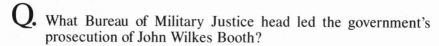

Q. What outspoken fighting man was promoted by Abraham Lincoln in spite of his having said the nation needed a military dictator?

A. Brig. Gen. Joseph Hooker (*b*. Massachusetts).

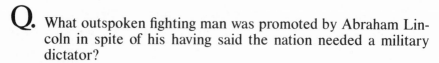

Q. The units that became the First, Second, Third, and Fifth California were raised in what city?

A. Philadelphia, Pennsylvania.

Q. Promoted to brigadier general before his twenty-first birthday, who was called the real hero of Fort Fisher and was awarded the Medal of Honor?

A. Galusha Pennypacker (*b*. Pennsylvania).

Q. What man is estimated to have recruited 10,000 unmarried men who were so young they were called babies?

A. Maj. Gen. Alvin Peterson Hovey (*b*. Indiana).

Q. What name was given to the Thirteenth Pennsylvania Reserves when the men began wearing on their hats the tails of deer?

A. Pennsylvania Bucktails.

Q. What notable contribution did a civilian, former Capt. Robert Parker Parrott, make to the war effort?

A. He invented the Parrott gun, one of the most widely used rifles.

*Admirers said the young Napoleon was a good title for George B. McClellan. Union cavalry swore by the handsome fellow who had invented the saddle in which they rode to battle; infantrymen believed in him fervently. Because he had a severe case of what Abraham Lincoln called "the slows," Mc-Clellan was not an outstanding commander. He opposed emancipation of slaves and, as Democratic nominee for the presidency in 1864, might have defeated Abraham Lincoln had it not been for Sherman's capture of Atlanta.*

[LIBRARY OF CONGRESS]

**Q.** What two future U.S. presidents served in the Twenty-third Ohio?

**A.** Brev. Maj. William McKinley and Brev. Maj. Gen. Rutherford B. Hayes.

◆

**Q.** A prewar artillery authority, what brigadier general attempted unsuccessfully throughout the war to make the artillery an independent branch of the service?

**A.** Henry Jackson Hunt (*b.* Michigan).

◆

**Q.** Men of what unit were largely responsible for digging the 500-foot-long Petersburg tunnel that permitted blowing up Confederate trenches, which formed The Crater?

**A.** The Forty-eighth Pennsylvania, comprised largely of coal miners from Schuylkill County.

◆

**Q.** Who commanded the famous Irish Brigade, made up of immigrants and first-generation Americans?

**A.** Brig. Gen. Thomas Francis Meagher (*b.* Ireland).

**Q.** What provost marshall of the Army of the Potomac survived all changes of command, McClellan through Grant?

**A.** Brig. Gen. Marsena Rudolph Patrick (*b*. New York).

---

**Q.** What Irishman was first on the list of hostages Confederates threatened to execute at Charleston, South Carolina, in November 1861?

**A.** Col. Michael Corcoran.

---

**Q.** When given command of the Department of the South in 1862, what general abolished slavery, an action President Lincoln nullified, stating he had exceeded his authority?

**A.** Maj. Gen. David Hunter (*b*. District of Columbia).

---

**Q.** What officer gained notoriety when he struck gunners with his saber "because of poor posture"?

**A.** Col. Richard Henry Jackson (*b*. Ireland).

---

**Q.** What millionaire soldier of fortune who was killed at Chantilly had a town in New Jersey and two decorations, a medal and a cross, named after him?

**A.** Maj. Gen. Philip Kearny (*b*. New York).

---

**Q.** After the war, what former general and U. S. senator ran for president on the Gold Democrat ticket, his vice presidential running mate being the former Confederate general Simon B. Buckner, his opponent at Chickamauga?

**A.** Maj. Gen. John McCauley Palmer (*b*. Kentucky).

---

**Q.** What major general and former congressman from Abraham Lincoln's home district was removed from command at Vicksburg when General Grant assumed personal command?

**A.** Maj. Gen. John A. McClernand (*b*. Kentucky).

# 3

# Roles of Civilians

Q. The parents of Thomas ("Tad") Lincoln became concerned because he had not learned to read at what age?

A. Nine.

————◆————

Q. After Shiloh, which Union general did Gov. David Todd of Ohio want court-martialed?

A. U. S. Grant.

————◆————

Q. What woman writer who defended Lincoln's use of war powers claimed to have planned the western campaign of 1862?

A. Anna Ella Carroll (*b.* Maryland).

————◆————

Q. Whose name is attached to a December 1860 proposal for six U.S. constitutional amendments regarding slavery, to seek sectional compromise to avoid war?

A. U.S. Sen. John J. Crittenden of Kentucky, proposer of the Crittenden Compromise.

————◆————

Q. What Scottish native reared in Alabama was enlisted in the Confederate army's medical department as a hospital matron?

A. Kate Cumming.

**Q.** What member of Lincoln's cabinet was appointed to the Supreme Court after resigning as secretary of the treasury following his unsuccessful attempt to win the 1864 Republican presidential nomination?

**A.** Salmon P. Chase (*b.* New Hampshire).

———◆———

**Q.** What outspoken pro-Unionist, through a Confederate congressman from Tennessee, tried to instigate his own unofficial peace talks with Abraham Lincoln in February 1865 but was rebuffed?

**A.** Henry S. Foote (*b.* Virginia).

———◆———

**Q.** Along with the Radical Republican senator Benjamin Wade, what Maryland congressman sponsored a harsh bill in 1864 aimed at thwarting Lincoln's "chicken-hearted" Reconstruction plans, which lead to a rare pocket veto by Lincoln?

**A.** Henry W. Davis (the Wade-Davis Bill).

———◆———

**Q.** What nurse, called "Dragon" by many subordinates, worked four years without pay as the Union's superintendent of women nurses?

**A.** Dorothea Lynde Dix (*b.* Maine).

———◆———

**Q.** What Ohio native and minstrel performer composed "Dixie" while living in New York City?

**A.** Daniel Decatur Emmett.

———◆———

**Q.** What secretary of war under President Buchanan was charged by Unionists after hostilities began with having sent huge quantities of military supplies to the South?

**A.** John B. Floyd of Virginia.

**Q.** What renowned Boston clergyman held a "slave auction" to buy the freedom of two adolescent girls?

**A.** Rev. Henry Ward Beecher of Plymouth Church.

———◆———

**Q.** What U.S. vice president framed the "nullification" doctrine that encouraged secessionists?

**A.** John C. Calhoun (*b*. South Carolina).

———◆———

**Q.** Widely accused of corruption in office, which one of Lincoln's cabinet members was called the "czar of Pennsylvania"?

**A.** Simon Cameron, secretary of war.

———◆———

**Q.** What member of Lincoln's 1861 cabinet was from west of the Mississippi River?

**A.** The attorney general, Edward Bates of Missouri (*b*. Virginia).

———◆———

**Q.** What member of a prominent Massachusetts family was chosen by Lincoln to serve in the vital post of minister to England, charged with preventing it from recognizing the South as an independent nation?

**A.** Charles Francis Adams, Sr.

———◆———

**Q.** Who was vice president of the Confederacy?

**A.** Alexander Hamilton Stephens (*b*. Georgia).

———◆———

**Q.** In 1863, what duly elected governor was prevented from being inaugurated because his state capital was occupied by Union troops?

**A.** Robert L. Caruthers of Tennessee.

[LIBRARY OF CONGRESS]

*In the aftermath of the bloodiest single day of the war at Antietam, Alexander Gardner managed to take many photographs of the dead. When they were placed on exhibition in New York City, they created a sensation. Gardner got scant praise at the time, however. As an employee of Matthew Brady, like everyone else on the staff of the man whose name is attached to thousands of Civil War photos, his work was exhibited under Brady's name. Not until years later was he credited with some of the most spine-chilling images made during the 1860s.*

[ALEXANDER GARDNER PHOTOGRAPH, LIBRARY OF CONGRESS]

*Confederate dead in the aftermath of battle.*

**Q.** What serious health problem was suffered by Edwin M. Stanton, U.S. secretary of war?

**A.** Asthma.

◆

**Q.** What Union spy, destined to gain fame for a daring railroad exploit, won the confidence of Confederates by smuggling quinine to them?

**A.** James J. Andrews (*b*. Virginia).

◆

**Q.** What two senators once accused General McClellan of plotting treason?

**A.** Benjamin F. Wade and Zachariah Chandler.

**Q.** What artist for *Frank Leslie's Illustrated Newspaper* sketched camp and battle scenes for thirty months?

**A.** Edwin Forbes (*b*. New York).

---

**Q.** What Confederate leader suffered from neuralgia and dyspepsia and was blind in one eye?

**A.** Jefferson Davis.

---

**Q.** What member of the Committee on the Conduct of the War initiated confiscation of southern property?

**A.** Zachariah Chandler of Michigan (*b*. New Hampshire).

---

**Q.** What conductor of the Underground Railroad has been called the "Moses of her people"?

**A.** Harriet Tubman.

---

**Q.** As U.S. secretary of war, what Confederate leader was responsible for forming the Camel Corps for desert service?

**A.** Jefferson Davis.

---

**Q.** When did Abraham Lincoln first meet his vice president, Hannibal Hamlin?

**A.** On Election Day, 1860.

---

**Q.** Who ordered the largest mass execution in American history, the hanging of thirty-eight Sioux Indians on December 26, 1862?

**A.** Abraham Lincoln.

Q. Who founded the Knights of the Golden Circle, an organization that attempted to influence public opinion in the North sympathetic to secession?

A. George Washington Lamb Bickley (*b*. Virginia).

---

### Who Said "Clothes Make the Man"?

The Reverend Henry Turner, pastor of the all-black Israel Beth congregation in Washington, D.C., put aside his clerical garb in order to recruit a regiment. As chaplain of the black unit, he kept the only detailed record of its activities.

Marching through coastal North Carolina, soldiers came to a sizable stream at the edge of a town. They took off their uniforms, attached them to their bayonets, and waded across. According to Turner, "dozens of white women in the finest attire imaginable" hurried to watch the first naked black men they had ever seen.

◆

James M. Mason, a Virginia aristocrat who went to England as a Confederate envoy, did not permit anyone— even his servants—to see him dressed informally. That is why he never came down to breakfast until after he had donned a dress coat.

◆

In the aftermath of battle, soldiers from both sides often swarmed over the field to loot the dead. A gold watch was seldom ignored, and any wallet full of currency went into the pocket of the finder. But more than gold or currency, those who scavenged among the fallen wanted a special prize: a good pair of shoes.

◆

Federal militia units poured into Washington in response to Abraham Lincoln's call for 75,000 volunteers. So many came so rapidly that a few arrived without trousers. Old capital hands solemnly reported that these fellows "were forced to go on duty or on parade in their drawers."

**Q.** What reporter from the Boston *Journal* is believed to have been the only war correspondent to cover the Civil War for all four years?

**A.** Charles Coffin (*b*. New Hampshire).

———————◆———————

**Q.** What small girl is generally credited with having persuaded Lincoln to grow a beard?

**A.** Grace Bedell, of Westfield, New York.

———————◆———————

**Q.** What Mexican War general and future president made futile objections to his daughter's marriage to Jefferson Davis?

**A.** Zachary Taylor.

———————◆———————

**Q.** Members of what religious groups were exempt from military service in the Confederacy upon payment of a five-hundred-dollar tax?

**A.** Dunkards, Mennonites, Nazarenes, and Quakers.

———————◆———————

**Q.** What Michigan-born battlefield nurse was awarded the Kearny Cross, normally given only to enlisted men of valor?

**A.** Annie Etheridge.

———————◆———————

**Q.** What American journalist and major short story writer drew on his realistic observations as a Civil War soldier in such well-known stories as "An Occurrence at Owl Creek Bridge"?

**A.** Ambrose Bierce.

———————◆———————

**Q.** Who was the only Jewish member of the group that functioned as a cabinet for Confederate president Jefferson Davis?

**A.** Judah P. Benjamin, department of war.

**Q.** What South Carolina aristocrat kept a journal that was later published as *A Diary from Dixie*?

**A.** Mary Boykin Miller Chesnut.

---

**Q.** What Confederate leader, a West Point graduate, colonel in the Mexican War, and former U.S. congressman, was an unsuccessful candidate for governor of Mississippi in 1851?

**A.** Jefferson Davis.

---

**Q.** What "photographer of the Confederacy" made a series of rare daguerreotypes showing the ironclads in action?

**A.** George S. Cook (*b.* Connecticut).

---

**Q.** In Lincoln's strongly Republican administration, what one-time Democrat served as U.S. secretary of war?

**A.** Edwin M. Stanton (*b.* Ohio).

---

**Q.** What raiders, captured by Confederates, were treated as civilian spies because they were out of uniform?

**A.** The twenty-four army volunteers who followed civilian James J. Andrews.

---

**Q.** What Confederate brigadier general resigned his commission to head the important Tredegar Iron Company in Richmond?

**A.** Joseph R. Anderson (*b.* Virginia).

---

**Q.** What civilian who ran one of the South's most successful hospitals was the only woman given a commission in the Confederate army?

**A.** Sally Tompkins (*b.* Virginia).

*Like Alexander Gardner, photographer George N. Barnard worked with equipment that today seems to have been incredibly slow and cumbersome. Here his darkroom tent is conspicuous on an Atlanta battlefield, with the rear of his wagon seen at the right of the photo. Barnard created one of the first comparatively complete photographic records of an army's movement—Sherman's Atlanta campaign.*

Q. Who is believed to have originated Lincoln's nickname, "the Original Gorilla"?

A. U.S. secretary of war Edwin M. Stanton.

———◆———

Q. What grandson of Thomas Jefferson, born at Monticello, was a cabinet member under Jefferson Davis?

A. George Wythe Randolph.

**Q.** As head of the Federal Secret Service, what espionage agent conducted a reign of terror in the North against suspected southern sympathizers?

**A.** Lafayette Curry Baker (*b*. New York).

———◆———

**Q.** The wartime photographs made by what famed photographer are now preserved in the Library of Congress?

**A.** Matthew Brady (*b*. Ireland).

———◆———

**Q.** What North Carolina governor opposed secession until Lincoln called for 75,000 volunteers?

**A.** John W. Ellis (*b*. North Carolina).

———◆———

**Q.** What wartime governor could not respond to Lincoln's call for troops after Fort Sumter because the state treasury was empty?

**A.** Austin Blair of Michigan (*b*. New York).

———◆———

**Q.** What Union governor was the first to respond to Lincoln's call for troops and subsequently raised a black regiment?

**A.** John Albion Andrew of Maine.

———◆———

**Q.** Whose poem, set to the tune of "John Brown's Body," remains even today one of the nation's most popular military songs?

**A.** Julia Ward Howe, author of "Battle Hymn of the Republic."

———◆———

**Q.** What Union captain and future U.S. Supreme Court justice, upon seeing a tall civilian—later identified as Abraham Lincoln—expose himself to bullets during enemy action yelled, "Get down, you fool!"?

**A.** Oliver Wendell Holmes, Jr. (*b*. Massachusetts).

**Q.** Respectable women attached to the army to perform various camp and nursing duties were known by what term?

**A.** Vivandières.

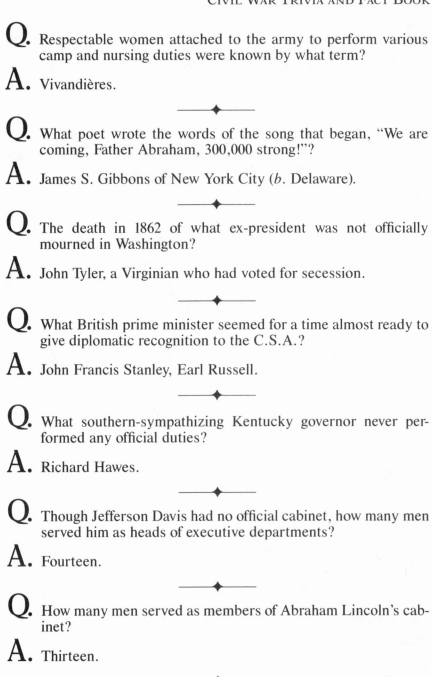

**Q.** What poet wrote the words of the song that began, "We are coming, Father Abraham, 300,000 strong!"?

**A.** James S. Gibbons of New York City (*b*. Delaware).

**Q.** The death in 1862 of what ex-president was not officially mourned in Washington?

**A.** John Tyler, a Virginian who had voted for secession.

**Q.** What British prime minister seemed for a time almost ready to give diplomatic recognition to the C.S.A.?

**A.** John Francis Stanley, Earl Russell.

**Q.** What southern-sympathizing Kentucky governor never performed any official duties?

**A.** Richard Hawes.

**Q.** Though Jefferson Davis had no official cabinet, how many men served him as heads of executive departments?

**A.** Fourteen.

**Q.** How many men served as members of Abraham Lincoln's cabinet?

**A.** Thirteen.

**Q.** What national hero was ousted from his post as governor because he refused to back secession for his state?

**A.** Sam Houston of Texas.

**Q.** After the election of 1864, the membership of what political group jumped by 70 percent?

**A.** Democratic members of the U.S. Congress, from forty-four members to seventy-five.

———◆———

**Q.** What Confederate governor was most stubborn in resisting legislation passed in Richmond?

**A.** Joseph Emerson Brown of Georgia.

———◆———

**Q.** Whose death in October 1862 caused Robert E. Lee to weep?

**A.** Ann Carter, age twenty-three, his second daughter.

———◆———

**Q.** What civilian is commemorated by a statue on the battlefield at Gettysburg?

**A.** John L. Burns, a seventy-four-year-old former cobbler who offered himself and his flintlock musket to Union forces.

———◆———

**Q.** What two cabinet members tried to force McClellan's resignation while Lincoln still relied upon him?

**A.** Edwin M. Stanton and Salmon P. Chase.

———◆———

**Q.** What British statesman in the fall of 1862 publicly stated secession would be successful?

**A.** William E. Gladstone, soon to be prime minister.

———◆———

**Q.** What prominent C.S.A. senator predicted defeat because of "overpowering numbers" of Federal troops?

**A.** Herschel V. Johnson of Georgia.

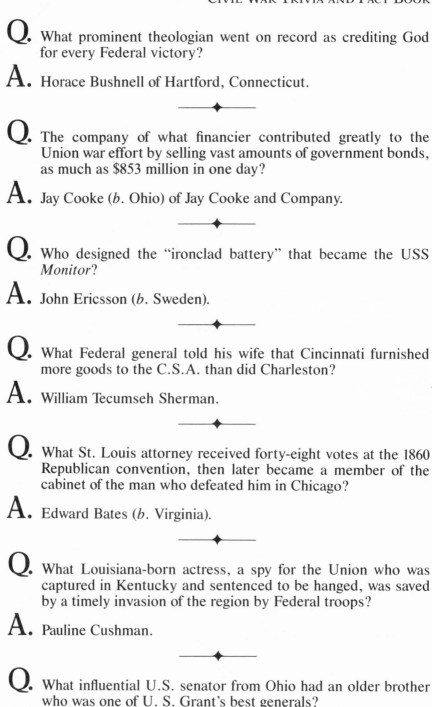

**Q.** What prominent theologian went on record as crediting God for every Federal victory?

**A.** Horace Bushnell of Hartford, Connecticut.

◆

**Q.** The company of what financier contributed greatly to the Union war effort by selling vast amounts of government bonds, as much as $853 million in one day?

**A.** Jay Cooke (*b.* Ohio) of Jay Cooke and Company.

◆

**Q.** Who designed the "ironclad battery" that became the USS *Monitor*?

**A.** John Ericsson (*b.* Sweden).

◆

**Q.** What Federal general told his wife that Cincinnati furnished more goods to the C.S.A. than did Charleston?

**A.** William Tecumseh Sherman.

◆

**Q.** What St. Louis attorney received forty-eight votes at the 1860 Republican convention, then later became a member of the cabinet of the man who defeated him in Chicago?

**A.** Edward Bates (*b.* Virginia).

◆

**Q.** What Louisiana-born actress, a spy for the Union who was captured in Kentucky and sentenced to be hanged, was saved by a timely invasion of the region by Federal troops?

**A.** Pauline Cushman.

◆

**Q.** What influential U.S. senator from Ohio had an older brother who was one of U. S. Grant's best generals?

**A.** John Sherman, later three times a presidential candidate, brother of Gen. William T. Sherman.

*Like Henry Wirz, Richard J. Gatling expected to spend his life as a family doctor. Unlike Wirz, when war broke out he remained with his patients. Always a handy fellow with tools and machinery, he designed several farm implements. Then he had an idea that led him to develop a rapid-fire gun that could deliver 250 rounds per minute. Dr. Gatling touted his new invention as "a great life-saving device, sure to bring wars to a speedy end" but failed to convince skeptics at the U.S. War Department. The Gatling gun was finally approved too late to see action during the Civil War. After serving for six years as president of the American Association of Inventors and Manufacturers, "humanitarian" Gatling devoted his last productive years to work on a mechanized plow.*

[*Dictionary of American Portraits*]

Q. What holder of high office was described by *Harper's Weekly* in December 1861 as being honest and shrewd but not a great leader?

A. Abraham Lincoln.

———◆———

Q. Why was the death of Brig. Gen. Benjamin Hardin Helm, C.S.A., mourned in the White House?

A. He was Mary Todd Lincoln's brother-in-law.

———◆———

Q. What frustrated head of the Confederate treasury resigned under pressure because he could not vitalize a faltering economy?

A. Christopher G. Memminger (*b*. Germany).

**Q.** With six secretaries of war in four years, why was the turnover so great in that Confederate department?

**A.** Excessive interference by President Davis, which caused frustration of the secretaries who were regarded as pawns.

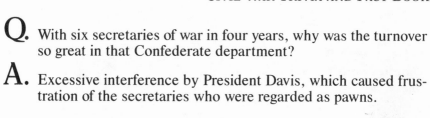

**Q.** What major American artist began his career as a news artist for *Harper's Weekly*, sketching battle and camp scenes?

**A.** Winslow Homer (*b*. Massachusetts).

**Q.** Based in Virginia, Capt. E. Porter Alexander was in charge of what special reconnaissance missions for the Confederacy in 1861–62?

**A.** Aerial observation with a gas-filled silk balloon.

**Q.** What political leader slipped into Washington by night, arriving very early on the morning of February 23, 1862?

**A.** Abraham Lincoln.

**Q.** How old was President Lincoln's son William Wallace ("Willie") when he died in the White House in 1862?

**A.** Eleven.

**Q.** How did Jefferson Davis spend the morning before his inauguration?

**A.** On his knees in prayer.

**Q.** Attempting to appease the governor, Democrat Reuben Fenton, Lincoln cut what state's draft quota by 25 percent?

**A.** New York.

**Q.** The first ironclad ships for Federal use were built in sixty-five days by what St. Louis contractor?

**A.** James B. Eads (*b*. Indiana).

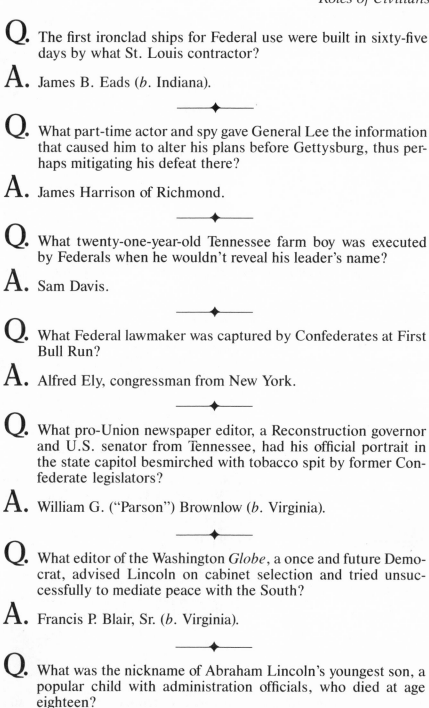

**Q.** What part-time actor and spy gave General Lee the information that caused him to alter his plans before Gettysburg, thus perhaps mitigating his defeat there?

**A.** James Harrison of Richmond.

**Q.** What twenty-one-year-old Tennessee farm boy was executed by Federals when he wouldn't reveal his leader's name?

**A.** Sam Davis.

**Q.** What Federal lawmaker was captured by Confederates at First Bull Run?

**A.** Alfred Ely, congressman from New York.

**Q.** What pro-Union newspaper editor, a Reconstruction governor and U.S. senator from Tennessee, had his official portrait in the state capitol besmirched with tobacco spit by former Confederate legislators?

**A.** William G. ("Parson") Brownlow (*b*. Virginia).

**Q.** What editor of the Washington *Globe*, a once and future Democrat, advised Lincoln on cabinet selection and tried unsuccessfully to mediate peace with the South?

**A.** Francis P. Blair, Sr. (*b*. Virginia).

**Q.** What was the nickname of Abraham Lincoln's youngest son, a popular child with administration officials, who died at age eighteen?

**A.** Thomas ("Tad") Lincoln, who was given his nickname by his father because at birth "he looked like a tadpole."

**Q.** Late in the war, draft protests in the Pennsylvania coal fields led to creation of what special force?

**A.** The Coal and Iron Police, used to curb dissent.

---

**Q.** Abraham Lincoln's eldest son, the only one to survive to adulthood, served Presidents Garfield and Arthur in what capacity?

**A.** Secretary of war.

---

**Q.** What former slave and author of a famed autobiography helped recruit blacks for the Union army and discussed problems of slavery with Abraham Lincoln?

**A.** Frederick Douglass (*b*. Maryland).

---

**Q.** Who was owner of the four gunboats seized at Fort Henry by Federal forces?

**A.** Builder James B. Eads.

---

**Q.** The melody of the popular Civil War ballad "Aura Lee" by George R. Poulton and W. W. Fosdick was later used for what twentieth-century hit song?

**A.** Elvis Presley's "Love Me Tender."

---

**Q.** What leader who ordered tens of thousands to their deaths was known to weep at reading "The Babes in the Woods"?

**A.** Jefferson Davis.

---

**Q.** Who was the only public advocate of reopening the slave trade soon after the war began?

**A.** C.S.A. senator William L. Yancey (*b*. Georgia).

**Q.** What admirer of General Sherman wrote "Marching Through Georgia," perhaps the most hated song in the South even today?

**A.** Henry C. Work.

---

**Q.** What former Kentucky governor and U.S. senator had two sons serving as major generals in the Civil War, one for the Union, the other for the Confederacy?

**A.** John J. Crittenden.

---

**Q.** Founder of the New York *Tribune,* what editor who signed the bail bond of Jefferson Davis was also one of Lincoln's earliest supporters?

**A.** Horace Greeley.

---

**Q.** What physician-inventor devised a weapon for the Union army, which used only twelve of them, that was the prototype of the machine gun?

**A.** Dr. Richard J. Gatling (*b*. North Carolina).

---

**Q.** Angered at not becoming postmaster general, what congressman joined the Radical Republican movement?

**A.** Henry W. Davis (*b*. Maryland).

---

**Q.** What key figure in the war typically addressed his wife as "Mother"?

**A.** Abraham Lincoln.

---

**Q.** What wife of a sergeant in the Fifth Rhode Island Infantry was regimental color-bearer at First Bull Run?

**A.** Kady Brownell (*b*. Africa).

**Q.** What professional photographer is remembered for his book, *Photographic Views of Sherman's Campaign*?

**A.** George N. Barnard (*b*. Connecticut).

---

**Q.** Who was the idealistic and fanatical abolitionist who left a prewar trail of blood in Kansas and Virginia?

**A.** John Brown (*b*. Connecticut).

---

**Q.** What did hundreds of northern admirers send General Grant after his victory at Fort Donelson?

**A.** Cigars.

---

**Q.** Who composed the popular song "When Johnny Comes Marching Home" in 1863?

**A.** Patrick Gilmore (stationed in occupied New Orleans).

---

**Q.** What Confederate leader attended Catholic schools even though his family was Baptist?

**A.** Jefferson Davis.

---

**Q.** What C.S.A. naval agent went abroad to purchase the *Florida*, the *Alabama*, and the *Shenandoah*?

**A.** James D. Bulloch (*b*. Georgia).

---

**Q.** What poet, a fervent admirer of Lincoln and a volunteer nurse, wrote *Leaves of Grass*?

**A.** Walter ("Walt") Whitman (*b*. New York).

---

**Q.** What was the maiden name of the First Lady of the Confederacy?

**A.** Varina Howell (*b*. Mississippi).

*Varina Howell became the second wife of 1st Lt. Jefferson Davis, U.S. Army, after the death of his first wife. Her husband fought with distinction in the Mexican War, served in the U.S. House of Representatives and the U.S. Senate, and in 1853 became secretary of war. While holding this cabinet post, he introduced camels in the West, hoping to improve the quality of life among troops that patrolled the deserts. Perfectly satisfied with her role as wife and mother, Mrs. Jefferson Davis wept in public when informed that she had suddenly become First Lady of the Confederate States of America.*

Q. Whose "Declaration of Immediate Causes" cited violations of the U.S. Constitution as the basis for secession?

A. Christopher G. Memminger (*b*. Germany).

◆

Q. What was the name of the "Irish Biddy" who marched with Philip Sheridan's men and may have fought with them?

A. Bridget Diver, or Deaver (*b*. Ireland).

Q. What Canadian woman successfully posed as a male nurse with the Second Michigan Infantry until threatened with exposure by illness?

A. Sarah Emma Edmonds (or Edmundson).

———◆———

Q. Who was Mrs. Robert E. Lee's famous great-grandmother?

A. Martha Washington.

———◆———

Q. What firm Unionist, who was appointed military governor of Tennessee, became the seventeenth president of the United States?

A. Andrew Johnson.

# 4

# Transportation and Communication

Q. Of the many signals transmitted to cavalry units by buglers, which one alerted them for march or combat?

A. "Boots and Saddles."

---

Q. Who was entrusted to deliver Lincoln's secret order relieving John C. Frémont of command in Missouri?

A. Leonard Swett, a political friend of the president.

---

Q. In what vehicle did Lt. Col. Robert E. Lee travel in 1861 from Fort Mason, Texas, to Washington?

A. An army ambulance.

---

Q. What was the difference between Union and Confederate directional bugle calls?

A. Practically none; they were almost identical.

---

Q. When Maj. Gen. Nathaniel Banks burned many freight cars following Cedar Mountain in August 1862, how did he move what was left of his supplies?

A. In horse-drawn wagons.

**Q.** On what transportation system was Sherman dependent during the Atlanta campaign?

**A.** The single-track Western and Atlantic Railroad.

---

**Q.** What important military message was found by the enemy after being used as a wrapper for cigars?

**A.** Lee's General Order No. 191, the famous Lost Order.

---

**Q.** What railroad crossed the Susquehanna River at Harrisburg, Pennsylvania?

**A.** The Pennsylvania Railroad.

---

**Q.** Whom did Robert E. Lee call the "eyes of the army," who "never brought me a piece of false information"?

**A.** Cavalry general J. E. B. Stuart.

---

**Q.** How were secret or detailed orders transmitted by a commander to subordinates at a distance?

**A.** By couriers on horseback who sometimes had to travel for miles.

---

**Q.** What was the shortest time required for a letter from San Antonio, Texas, to reach Washington?

**A.** Ten days.

---

**Q.** When the assistant secretary of the navy, Gustavus Fox, feared that orders for the Federal fleet in the Mississippi River might not reach their destination, what did he do?

**A.** He sent triplicate orders on three ships.

Q. What noted Confederate leader refused to write a letter that would be in transit on Sunday?

A. Stonewall Jackson.

---

Q. When he was ordered to Washington from western Virginia by President Lincoln on July 22, 1861, how long did it take General McClellan to travel the distance?

A. Four days, on horseback and by rail.

---

Q. How did a naval officer let it be known that his ship was ready for action against the enemy?

A. The "attack" pennant was hoisted.

---

Q. On June 9, 1862, when Maj. Gen. Henry Halleck telegraphed President Lincoln that he had ordered Don Carlos Buell to go on the attack, what was the response?

A. "Greatly delighted."

---

Q. What was the signal, transmitted by drum or bugle, by which a commander ordered scattered forces to regroup?

A. "Rally."

---

Q. How many transportation units did C.S.A. General John H. Morgan confiscate during a raid on Lexington, Kentucky?

A. Seven thousand horses.

---

Q. What was the most active and successful Southern port for blockade running?

A. Wilmington, North Carolina.

**Q.** What all-important railroad led from Wilmington, North Carolina, to Richmond, Virginia?

**A.** The Wilmington and Weldon Railroad.

———◆———

**Q.** Though not a word might be said, what message was communicated when cooked rations for three days were issued?

**A.** "Prepare to attack."

———◆———

**Q.** What commercial agency delivered mail in both the North and the South for several months after Fort Sumter?

**A.** The American Express Letter Company.

———◆———

**Q.** For as long as a letter could be sent from one warring region to another, what was the cost?

**A.** Twenty-five cents.

———◆———

**Q.** What Federal commander habitually bypassed Gen. Winfield Scott, communicating directly with Lincoln and members of his cabinet?

**A.** George B. McClellan.

———◆———

**Q.** What Confederate general had on his staff a wire-tap expert who sometimes penetrated the Federal telegraph network?

**A.** Cavalryman-raider John Hunt Morgan.

———◆———

**Q.** What Federal commander ordered that any civilian who attempted to communicate with the enemy would be put to death?

**A.** Gen. John Pope, labeled "the miscreant Pope" by Lee.

[L. & N. RAILROAD]

*If not the most famous of Civil War locomotives, Old No. 9 set a record that stood for decades. Chasing a stolen engine used by James J. Andrews and his raiders, Confederates in the locomotive, formally known as the* Texas, *achieved speeds of at least seventy miles per hour, running backward. Nothing quite like this exploit was done again for many years. In 1912, noted artist Wilbur G. Kurtz of Atlanta produced a splendid water color depicting the engine that ran backward in pursuit of the stolen* General.

Q. With commanders usually at a distance from the site of conflict, how did they order their men to fall back?

A. "Retreat" was sounded by bugles or drums.

◆

Q. What important visitor did General McClellan deliberately shun in November 1861 by going to bed instead of seeing him?

A. Abraham Lincoln.

**Q.** How many copies of Lee's Special Order No. 191, the famous Lost Order, reached their destinations safely?

**A.** Six.

---

**Q.** How did General Lee usually transmit reports from the field to Jefferson Davis in Richmond?

**A.** By letter.

---

**Q.** Until "Taps" replaced it for Federal troops in 1862, what bugle call signified the end of the day at 10:00 P.M.?

**A.** "Tattoo."

---

**Q.** When Lee considered it imperative that Magruder understand orders for Malvern Hill, what did he do?

**A.** He rode to Savage's Station to explain them in person.

---

**Q.** In one of his letters, whom did General McClellan characterize as simply "a teller of low stories"?

**A.** Abraham Lincoln.

---

**Q.** When McClellan was removed from command of the Army of the Potomac, how did he get word of the demotion?

**A.** From a day-old newspaper.

---

**Q.** Who served as director of railroad transportation for Federal armies in the east for sixteen months?

**A.** Herman Haupt (*b.* Pennsylvania).

---

**Q.** What signal, transmitted by drum, ordered sailors to go below decks?

**A.** "Beat-to-Quarters."

Q. What was the approximate effective range of the mobile telegraph widely used by Union forces?

A. Five miles.

◆

Q. While in camp, what was the maximum number of bugle calls a
Union soldier could expect to hear in a day?

A. Nineteen.

◆

Q. Ordered in May 1862 to move against Stonewall Jackson, General McClellan required how long to advance seventy miles?

A. About eight days.

◆

Q. When Federal troops moved across the Rappahannock River
on December 11, 1862, what prearranged signal warned Lee?

A. Two cannons were fired at 4:45 A.M.

◆

Q. What vital supply line crossed the river at Harpers Ferry, Virginia (now West Virginia)?

A. The Baltimore and Ohio Railroad.

◆

Q. What communication system did President Lincoln suggest for
military use in June 1862?

A. "Beacons of smoke by day and fires by night."

◆

Q. How did C.S.A. lieutenant general Richard Taylor manage to
sleep while traveling cross country?

A. He slept in an ambulance pulled by trained mules.

◆

Q. How long did it take Grant's June 1863 telegram of dismissal to
reach John A. McClernand?

A. Eleven days.

Q. When there was no time for writing orders during battle, what was a common means of communicating?

A. Oral orders were transmitted by courier.

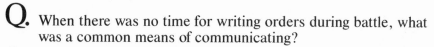

Q. Before starting on a long and hazardous march, what Union commander cut telegraph lines to sever communication with superiors so the enemy would not be able to intercept any messages?

A. William Tecumseh Sherman, launching the March to the Sea.

Q. With photo technology in its infancy, how did the news media usually illustrate their battlefield dispatches?

A. With woodblock engravings of artists' sketches.

Q. The seizure of what rail line did President Lincoln consider in June 1862 to be "as important as the taking of Richmond"?

A. ". . . the railroad at or east of Cleveland, Tennessee."

Q. In July 1862, what official checked and sometimes altered telegrams sent to the president and the secretary of war?

A. The supervisor of military telegrams.

Q. Who informed President Lincoln on June 30, 1862, that, after days of fighting, most Federal forces were safely south of the Chickahominy River?

A. A newspaper reporter who had talked with a paymaster.

Q. With lanterns widely used as signal devices, what colors were usually employed?

A. Red and white.

**Q.** What caused Maj. Gen. John Pope to lose communication with Washington in August 1862?

**A.** Enemy forces cut his telegraph lines.

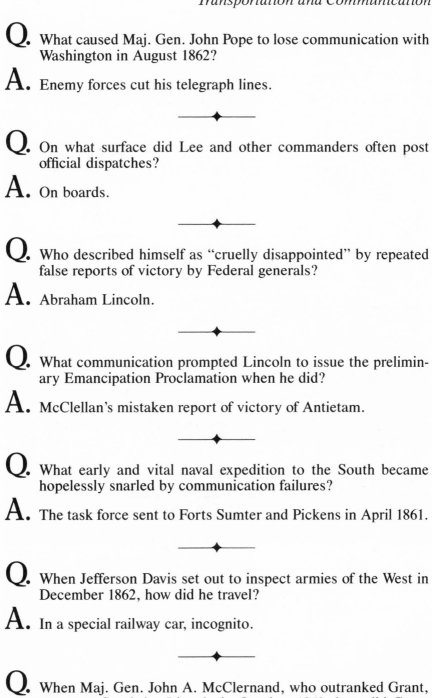

**Q.** On what surface did Lee and other commanders often post official dispatches?

**A.** On boards.

**Q.** Who described himself as "cruelly disappointed" by repeated false reports of victory by Federal generals?

**A.** Abraham Lincoln.

**Q.** What communication prompted Lincoln to issue the preliminary Emancipation Proclamation when he did?

**A.** McClellan's mistaken report of victory of Antietam.

**Q.** What early and vital naval expedition to the South became hopelessly snarled by communication failures?

**A.** The task force sent to Forts Sumter and Pickens in April 1861.

**Q.** When Jefferson Davis set out to inspect armies of the West in December 1862, how did he travel?

**A.** In a special railway car, incognito.

**Q.** When Maj. Gen. John A. McClernand, who outranked Grant, was sent South by Lincoln in October 1862, how did Grant learn of it?

**A.** By putting together rumors found in newspaper stories.

Q. When Burnside urgently appealed to Washington for pontoons in November 1862, how long did it take for them to arrive at Falmouth, Virginia?

A. Eight days, thus enabling Lee to move to Fredericksburg.

———◆———

Q. Later the famed editor of the New York *Sun*, what journalist was assigned by Secretary of War Stanton as a special investigating agent, submitting frequent reports on the conduct of General Grant?

A. Charles A. Dana.

———◆———

Q. At what three paces did buglers of marching cavalry units, North and South, keep the cavalry moving?

A. "Walk," "Canter," and "Trot."

———◆———

Q. What bridge did Confederate raiders find "indestructible" when they tried to burn it?

A. The railroad bridge over the Conochocheague River, Pennsylvania.

———◆———

Q. What famed transportation route crossed the Blue Ridge Mountains at Turner's Gap, Kentucky?

A. The National Road.

———◆———

Q. How did Stonewall Jackson typically begin messages in which he reported victories?

A. "Through God's blessing . . ."

———◆———

Q. Having studied Indian smoke signals, deaf-mute alphabets, and the Morse code, U.S. Army surgeon Albert J. Myer devised what new signal technique?

A. The "wigwag," using flags by day and torches by night.

*Having come to Chicago from his native Scotland, Allan Pinkerton found work as a maker of barrels. When counterfeit currency began floating around the city, he became an amateur detective and broke up the ring. So he quit working as a cooper and opened one of the nation's first detective services. Because Abraham Lincoln had received death threats, friends hired him to guard the president-elect on his journey to the capital. Soon he became chief of intelligence for the Army of the Potomac. He and his agents gathered great quantities of information but showed little capacity to analyze it. Pinkerton's highly inflated estimates of Confederate strength sometimes helped persuade Gen. George B. McClellan to retreat when he should have attacked.*

**Q.** When McClellan reported having dispersed Lee's army in September 1862, who responded, "God bless you; destroy the rebel army if possible"?

**A.** Abraham Lincoln.

Q. At Frayser's Farm, what was Lee's only source of information about progress of the battle?

A. His eyes.

---

Q. What was the bugle call that was heard most often about sunrise?

A. "Reveille."

---

Q. In battle, while the cavalry and artillery relied on buglers for directive signals, whom did the infantry rely on for directions of maneuvers?

A. Drummers.

---

Q. What notable C.S.A strategist typically refused to inform top aides about forthcoming movements?

A. Stonewall Jackson.

---

Q. Traveling behind both Union and Confederate lines, the celebrated artist-correspondent Frank Vizetelly covered the Civil War for what foreign publication?

A. *Illustrated London News.*

---

Q. What Federal commander made elaborate plans to cross the Rappahannock River, but kept them secret from his own subordinates?

A. Maj. Gen. Joseph Hooker.

---

Q. What Federal office was described as "haunted by Lincoln day and night—often very late"?

A. The telegraph office of the War Department.

## Bones, Bones, and More Bones

After John B. Hood, a leader of questionable ability who became a favorite of Jefferson Davis, lost a leg in combat, he found a splendid French-made cork leg as a replacement. He liked it so well that he never climbed aboard a horse without it. A man of caution, Hood always carried a second cork leg dangling from his saddle.

At Gettysburg, Dan Sickles was knocked from his saddle when a cannon ball scored a direct hit. Within a half-hour, a Union surgeon had amputated the mangled leg, but Sickles did not lose interest in it. At his direction, splintered bones were sent to the Army Medical Museum in Washington, D.C., where the colorful major general paid periodic visits to them.

Only minutes away from Sickles's trophies, all the bones of Major General Joseph Wheeler lie in Arlington National Cemetery. They are there because the Georgia native was one of the few ex-Confederates to hold high command during the Spanish-American War.

Q. When he was ordered from Richmond to Chattanooga late in 1862, how long was Joseph E. Johnston's journey to his new post?

A. Five days, by train.

———◆———

Q. Although several telegrams went to Washington in the aftermath of Chancellorsville, who failed to learn the outcome of the battle that day?

A. Abraham Lincoln.

———◆———

Q. When Lee called for a general advance at Malvern Hill, why were General Magruder's troops not in their assigned places?

A. Magruder had been given misdirections for marching by local guides.

By the time Confederates fired upon Fort Sumter, editors of many weekly newspapers had decided to give visual coverage to the growing conflict. Photography blossomed during the four years of war but never made other art forms obsolete. Battlefield artists often made on-the-spot sketches and sent them to their editors. Skilled artisans then used blocks of very hard wood to carve mirror images of scenes chosen for publication. "Wash Day" shows that every good stream proved enticing to grimy fighting men. Since wood did not lend itself to fine details often associated with engravings upon metal, many lines of a good wood engraving are relatively broad and straight.

Q. When did the telegram announcing the Federal victory at Vicksburg, Mississippi, on July 4, 1863, actually reach Washington?

A. On July 7.

**Q.** What epochal document signed by Lincoln was destroyed by fire at the State Department?

**A.** The Emancipation Proclamation.

———◆———

**Q.** What Federal commander so despised newspaper reporters that he was said to foam at the mouth upon seeing one?

**A.** William Tecumseh Sherman.

———◆———

**Q.** What faraway newspaper denounced the Emancipation Proclamation as a hypocritical sham?

**A.** The London *Spectator*.

———◆———

**Q.** How did the London *Times*, rival of the *Spectator*, describe Lincoln's edict that freed slaves in rebel territory?

**A.** That newspaper termed it "a very sad document."

———◆———

**Q.** How far did Lee's messenger ride when sent to A. P. Hill at Harpers Ferry, before Sharpsburg?

**A.** Seventeen miles.

———◆———

**Q.** With communication between Lincoln and his generals often snarled, what new office was created to facilitate flow of messages between him and Grant?

**A.** Chief of staff, with Gen. Henry Halleck serving there first.

———◆———

**Q.** Wishing to consult retired general Winfield Scott, what did Abraham Lincoln do?

**A.** He took a train to West Point to talk with him.

———◆———

**Q.** Approximately how long did it take to reach Corinth, Mississippi, from Memphis, Tennessee, on horseback?

**A.** Three days.

[*Leslie's Illustrated Weekly*]

Q. What was the size of railroad trestles at Muldraugh's Hill, Kentucky, destroyed by John Hunt Morgan, C.S.A., in December 1862?

A. They were eighty feet tall and five hundred feet long.

------◆------

Q. What city was the hub of every railroad linking Richmond with the eastern Confederacy?

A. Petersburg, Virginia.

------◆------

Q. How long did it take the army of Braxton Bragg to go the 150 miles from Chattanooga to Glasgow, Kentucky, in 1862?

A. Seventeen days.

------◆------

Q. Because of transportation costs, what did peaches that sold for two cents in Charleston bring in Richmond?

A. Twenty cents or more.

------◆------

Q. The actions of what general caused the Confederate Congress to propose punishment for newspapers that gave detailed military information?

A. Robert E. Lee, who regularly gleaned much useful information from the Philadelphia *Inquirer*, thought Northern generals might be following a similar practice.

------◆------

Q. What message to the nation was framed and transmitted in the aftermath of the fall of Atlanta?

A. Lincoln's "Order of Thanks and Rejoicing," September 3, 1864.

------◆------

Q. What Christmas gift was announced to President Lincoln by means of an 1864 telegram?

A. The city of Savannah, Georgia, and 25,000 bales of cotton, presented by William T. Sherman.

**Q.** With no overall policy for censorship of the press, the Union army relied on what means to control release of military information?

**A.** Self-censorship directed by the commanding generals.

———◆———

**Q.** What famous gaffe was committed by the Associated Press correspondent at First Bull Run?

**A.** Leaving the battlefield early to report the Union "victory," he had to get his information about the defeat from civilian refugees.

———◆———

**Q.** What railroad ran within 500 yards of Tennessee's Cumberland River at some points?

**A.** The Louisville and Nashville.

———◆———

**Q.** When mail transported to front-line Federal units was delayed, what rumor frequently spread as a result?

**A.** "Glory be! The war is over!"

———◆———

**Q.** With Federal troops in retreat near Perryville, Kentucky, in October 1862, what important transportation unit was captured?

**A.** An ammunition train of fifteen heavily loaded wagons.

———◆———

**Q.** What transportation system linked Richmond with the South Atlantic states?

**A.** The Weldon Railroad.

———◆———

**Q.** What famed political cartoonist influenced public opinion in favor of the North through his wartime work for *Harper's Weekly*?

**A.** Thomas Nast.

**Q.** How many miles of the Baltimore and Ohio Railroad were torn up during the Antietam campaign?

**A.** About thirty-five miles.

———◆———

**Q.** What newspaper was widely considered to be the most "anti-Richmond publication of the C.S.A."?

**A.** The Charleston *Mercury*, Robert B. Rhett, Jr., editor.

———◆———

**Q.** The long, shrill battle cry voiced by attacking Confederates that struck fear in the hearts of the enemy became known by what designation?

**A.** The Rebel yell.

———◆———

**Q.** What was the inflated wartime price of *Harper's Weekly*, the nationally circulated pro-Union illustrated newspaper?

**A.** Six cents per copy.

———◆———

**Q.** The editors of what newspaper ignorant of the South habitually referred to "Fort Sumpter" in headlines?

**A.** The New York *Times*.

———◆———

**Q.** What signal was used throughout the North and the South to notify the general public of portentous war news?

**A.** Ringing of church bells.

———◆———

**Q.** At what point in Kentucky were 4,000 Federal troops stationed as guards during much of 1862?

**A.** At the Louisville and Nashville Railroad crossing of the Green River.

Harpers Ferry, a remote mountain village in what is now West Virginia, took its name from an early boat used to cross a river. Later it became a transportation hub served by railroads and river boats. At that time the tiny settlement was much like a modern town suddenly made the point of intersection of three interstate highways. Because it was such an important transportation hub, it was chosen as the site for a huge U.S. Army depot. Weapons in that depot drew abolitionist John Brown who, with his surviving men, was captured by a strike force commanded by Lt. Col. Robert E. Lee of the U.S. Army.

**Q.** How did Abraham Lincoln learn in 1860 that he was the Republican nominee for the presidency?

**A.** By a telegram sent from Chicago to Springfield.

◆

**Q.** The Civil War was the last major conflict in which each regiment had what affiliate group to inspire it in combat?

**A.** A military band.

*Allan Pinkerton*, left, *conveys late word about Confederate forces to Gen. George B. McClellan, commander of the Army of the Potomac.*

Q. When did a twenty-four-hour delay in receiving orders prevent Leonidas Polk, C.S.A., from obeying Braxton Bragg?

A. October 8, 1862, advancing toward Frankfort, Kentucky.

---◆---

Q. On retreat from Kentucky in October 1862, what vehicles used by Braxton Bragg to haul supplies were conspicuous?

A. Four hundred captured wagons with "U.S." stenciled on them.

---◆---

Q. Who invented for Union forces a mobile telegraph system whose operators did not have to know the Morse code?

A. George W. Beardslee, the "magneto-electric field telegraph."

Q. Maj. Thomas T. Eckert of what military service suppressed General Grant's order to remove General Thomas from command long enough to allow Thomas to win the battle of Nashville?

A. Military Telegraph Service.

———◆———

Q. When troops were moved by rail through the South, why did they have to detrain, then board another train at state lines?

A. Southern states had different rail gauges.

———◆———

Q. How many different railroad companies were in operation in the southern states?

A. 112.

———◆———

Q. When Gen. James Longstreet arrived at Catoosa Station to reinforce Confederates at the battle of Chickamauga, how did he locate the battlefield?

A. With no guide awaiting him, he followed the sounds of the fighting.

———◆———

Q. Upon seizing a telegraph office in Kentucky, what mischievous Confederate cavalry officer wired countermand orders rescinding Union general Jeremiah Boyle's instructions to pursue him?

A. John Hunt Morgan.

[LESLIE'S ILLUSTRATED WEEKLY]

# 5

# First Events and Achievements

Q. Who was the first general to be replaced by Lincoln, having been earlier picked by Lincoln to command?

A. Irvin McDowell, replaced by McClellan.

———◆———

Q. What was the target of the first military attack ever made on an oil installation?

A. Burning Springs, Virginia, named for burning oil.

———◆———

Q. In what year did the city of Vicksburg, Mississippi, first celebrate the Fourth of July after it fell to General Grant on July 4, 1863?

A. 1945, with a larger celebration in 1947 attended by Gen. Dwight D. Eisenhower.

———◆———

Q. Who received the first Congressional Medal of Honor?

A. Pvt. Jacob Parott, a member of the Andrews' Raiders team that tried to wreck the Atlantic and Western Railroad north of Atlanta.

———◆———

Q. Connecticut-born George S. Smith of Charleston, South Carolina, made an epochal first photograph of what?

A. Ironclads, the USS *Weehawken*, *Montauk*, *Passaic*, in action firing on Fort Moultrie, South Carolina, September 8, 1863.

*Considerable evidence suggests that Abraham Lincoln deliberately provoked insurgents into firing upon Fort Sumter so that the Union would not be perceived as having started the war. Whatever the case, the artillery duel between the Federal installation and shore batteries involved an exchange of tens of thousands of shells. Incredibly, not a single fatality resulted. Only one member of the Fort Sumter garrison died when a big gun exploded during surrender ceremonies.*

Q. Where was U. S. Grant's first big failure in the campaign to open the Mississippi River?

A. Vicksburg, Mississippi, in 1862.

———◆———

Q. The first time in military history that a railroad was used for strategic mobility was when Confederate general Joseph E. Johnston moved his troops for what battle?

A. First Bull Run, July 18, 1861.

———◆———

Q. Where did a Union photographer first take a photo of C.S.A. fighting men?

A. At Fredericksburg in December 1862, by a Brady studio member.

———◆———

Q. What naval officer is believed to have been the first to order the Fourth of July celebrated by a twenty-one-gun salute?

A. Capt. David G. Farragut, 1862.

———◆———

Q. Who was the first man in the U.S. military to hold the rank of general of the army?

A. U. S. Grant.

———◆———

Q. When the first duel between ironclads took place on February 25, 1862, how long did the inconclusive battle last?

A. About four hours.

———◆———

Q. What Harvard Medical School graduate was the first black field officer?

A. Maj. Martin R. Delany, attached to a regiment stationed at Charleston, South Carolina.

Baltimore, Maryland, was the site of the first fatalities resulting from shots fired in anger. Members of the Sixth Massachusetts Infantry, headed toward Washington to help defend it, were taunted by prosecession civilians on April 19, 1861. No one ever confessed to having fired the first shot, but Federal guns were turned upon civilians armed only with clubs and stones. The ensuing melee resulted in at least fifteen deaths and dozens of injuries. Weeks passed before a military engagement led to a comparable number of casualties.

Q. Where did Union cavalry win the first significant victory over Confederate cavalry?

A. At Kelly's Ford, Virginia, March 17, 1863.

—————◆—————

Q. What American Indian was first to serve as military secretary to a commanding general?

A. Col. Ely Parker, secretary to U. S. Grant.

**Q.** Who was the first general officer, Union or Confederate, to die on the battlefield?

**A.** Brig. Gen. Robert S. Garnett, C.S.A., died July 13, 1861, at Corrick's Ford, Virginia.

———◆———

**Q.** When canned rations were first distributed for army fare, what derogatory name did Union soldiers give to canned beef?

**A.** Embalmed beef.

———◆———

**Q.** Where was the "Rebel yell" believed to have been used for the first time in battle?

**A.** At First Bull Run (First Manassas), July 21, 1861.

———◆———

**Q.** Who made the first purchase of Gatling machine guns, at $1,000 each?

**A.** Maj. Gen. Benjamin F. Butler, who bought twelve.

———◆———

**Q.** Where was the first post of the Grand Army of the Republic organized?

**A.** Springfield, Illinois, April 1, 1866.

———◆———

**Q.** Who received the first battlefield promotion of the war?

**A.** Arnold Elzey, C.S.A., from colonel to brigadier general, July 21, 1861.

———◆———

**Q.** When did northern newspapers first report the sighting of Confederate observation balloons?

**A.** June 1861, in the vicinity of Big Bethel, Virginia.

———◆———

**Q.** Where did Union forces win their first victory in a major battle?

**A.** At Fort Donelson, Tennessee, February 13–16, 1862.

**Q.** Who was the commander in chief of Union forces after the resignation of Winfield Scott?

**A.** George B. McClellan, November 5, 1861.

———✦———

**Q.** Who was the first commander of the Union Army of Virginia?

**A.** John Pope, June 26, 1862.

———✦———

**Q.** What was the first major battle in which black troops actively participated for the Union?

**A.** Port Hudson, Louisiana, May 27, 1863.

———✦———

**Q.** Who was the highest ranking civilian to volunteer for military service during the Civil War?

**A.** Hannibal Hamlin, vice president of the United States.

———✦———

**Q.** What was the first Federal warship to blockade a Southern port?

**A.** The *Sabine*, at Pensacola, Florida, April 1861.

———✦———

**Q.** What civilian was the first female casualty of all-out battle?

**A.** Mrs. Judith Henry, hit by a shell on July 21, 1861.

———✦———

**Q.** Who was the source of Union strategy at the beginning of the war to hold Fort Monroe, extend the blockade, guard Washington, and take Charleston, South Carolina?

**A.** President Abraham Lincoln.

———✦———

**Q.** Where did former Virginia Military Institute professor Stonewall Jackson claim victory despite major losses?

**A.** At Cedar Mountain, Virginia, August 9, 1862.

*Demand for cotton had declined because of high cost until Eli Whitney of Connecticut invented the cotton gin. Once cotton became a staple of world commerce, use of slave labor in the Cotton Belt increased in dramatic fashion. Bales piled on a wharf at Savannah, Georgia, were intended for the cotton mills of England. Yet the need for it in England and Europe did not bring foreign nations to the aid of the Confederate States of America. Huge quantities were burned, production lagged due to the pressure of military needs, and prices actually declined during the war. Instead of serving as the key to Southern independence, labor-intensive cotton production proved to be a millstone around the neck of the C.S.A.*

Q. The South's first organized secret-service bureau, formed in 1862, was part of what larger organization?

A. The C.S.A. Signal Corps.

**Q.** What was the first decoration presented to black fighting men?

**A.** The Butler Medal, purchased by Gen. Benjamin F. Butler in May 1865, when he prepared to run for Congress.

---

**Q.** What port was first on the list of naval targets prepared by Lincoln in early October 1861?

**A.** Port Royal, South Carolina.

---

**Q.** When was the Union's Western Department, extending from Ohio west, first formed?

**A.** July 3, 1861, with John Charles Frémont, commander.

---

**Q.** In July 1862 what force sent 35,000 men by train from Tupelo, Mississippi, to Chattanooga, Tennessee?

**A.** The Confederate Army of the Mississippi (Braxton Bragg).

---

**Q.** Who was the first presidential candidate of the newly formed Republican Party in 1856?

**A.** Future Maj. Gen. John Charles Frémont.

---

**Q.** What officer was first to be placed in charge of a Confederate department?

**A.** Maj. Gen. David E. Twiggs, spring 1861.

---

**Q.** When did Congress first authorize a Medal of Honor for enlisted men of the U.S. Navy and Marine Corps?

**A.** December 21, 1861.

---

**Q.** Who was first in seniority among officers commanding volunteer units fighting for the Union?

**A.** Maj. Gen. John A. Dix, commissioned May 16, 1861.

**Q.** From what site did the first recorded aerial reconnaissance originate?

**A.** From decks of the USS *Fanny*, August 3, 1861.

———◆———

**Q.** Who was first to be generally recognized as a double agent, working simultaneously for the North and South?

**A.** Timothy Webster, arrested in Richmond in April 1862.

———◆———

**Q.** When was suspension of *habeas corpus* first legalized by act of Congress?

**A.** March 1863, two years after Lincoln's presidential proclamation suspended it.

———◆———

**Q.** Who was the first person to receive the Congressional Medal of Honor twice?

**A.** Lt. Thomas Custer, brother of George A. Custer.

———◆———

**Q.** Where did the first modern naval battle between ironclad vessels take place?

**A.** Hampton Roads, Virginia, March 8, 1862.

———◆———

**Q.** What Confederate was first to be promoted to the rank of full general?

**A.** P. T. G. Beauregard, August 31, 1861 (backdated to June 21, 1861).

———◆———

**Q.** Who was the first member of the Republican party to become president?

**A.** Abraham Lincoln.

———◆———

**Q.** When was the first Jewish chaplain appointed by Abraham Lincoln?

**A.** September 1862, after months of congressional debate.

---◆---

**Q.** When did Abraham Lincoln first meet with Confederate commissioners who wanted to talk peace?

**A.** February 3, 1865, at Hampton Roads, Virginia.

---◆---

**Q.** Who gave the first battlefield promotion as a reward for "distinguished conduct"?

**A.** Jefferson Davis, at First Bull Run.

---◆---

**Q.** What battle was first to be personally observed by a head of state?

**A.** First Bull Run (by Jefferson Davis).

---◆---

**Q.** Having been made inspector general of the District of Columbia, who claimed to be the first person mustered into service to fight secession?

**A.** Brig. Gen. Charles P. Stone, January 2, 1861.

---◆---

**Q.** Where was the first C.S.A. military prison, a converted three-story tobacco barn?

**A.** Richmond, Virginia.

---◆---

**Q.** Who was first to permit fleeing John Wilkes Booth to pass a guard station?

**A.** Sgt. Silas T. Cobb, at the Navy Yard bridge.

---◆---

**Q.** Where was the first gun fired in defense of the Union?

**A.** At Pensacola, Florida, January 8, 1861, when state troops occupied federal forts.

**Q.** What was the first—and only—military medal awarded in the Confederacy?

**A.** The Davis Guard Medal, given by residents of Sabine City, Texas, to the Davis Guards, a military company.

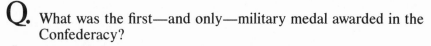

**Q.** Who was the only man killed at Fort Sumter?

**A.** Pvt. Daniel Hough, killed by accidental explosion, April 14, 1861.

**Q.** What Union commander was first to receive significant information from observation balloons?

**A.** Ambrose P. Burnside, near Fredericksburg, Virginia, December 1862.

**Q.** What Virginian is widely believed to have fired the first shot against Fort Sumter?

**A.** Edmund Ruffin, whose claim is highly questionable.

**Q.** Where did the first Confederate Congress meet?

**A.** Montgomery, Alabama.

**Q.** When did officers of the U.S. Army first become eligible to receive the Congressional Medal of Honor?

**A.** March 3, 1863, seven months after enlisted men were eligible.

**Q.** From what point was the first shot fired against Fort Sumter?

**A.** From a battery on James Island.

**Q.** As postwar president of Washington College in Lexington, Virginia, Robert E. Lee created the nation's first departments in what two curricula fields?

**A.** Journalism and commerce.

[BATTLES AND LEADERS OF THE CIVIL WAR]

*Allen C. Redwood sketched Confederate troops piled on top of boxcars, as well as into them, for their crucial journey to the hamlet of Manassas. Union forces named the ensuing battle of July 1861 for Bull Run Creek, which drained the area.*

Q. What Indian tribe was the first to declare its loyalty to the C.S.A.?

A. The Choctaws, who passed such a resolution on February 7, 1861.

—◆—

Q. What clash of at least 100,000 men is often termed "the first great modern battle"?

A. Shiloh, April 6–7, 1862.

—◆—

Q. When did the C.S.A. enact its first national conscription law?

A. April 16, 1862.

**Q.** What body of uniformed black troops is believed to have been first to organize and drill?

**A.** The First South Carolina Volunteers, summer 1862.

---

**Q.** What Union officer was the North's "first martyr of the war"?

**A.** Col. Ephraim Elmer Ellsworth, Eleventh New York, May 24, 1861.

---

**Q.** What Federal officer was the first to be arrested and imprisoned on order of the Committee on the Conduct of the War?

**A.** Brig. Gen. Charles P. Stone, who never was informed of the charges that had been leveled against him.

---

**Q.** Crewmen of what ship were the first considered to be guilty of piracy?

**A.** The Confederate privateer *Savannah*.

---

**Q.** After the war, what was the first state to be readmitted into the Union?

**A.** Tennessee, July 24, 1866.

---

**Q.** What civilian did Confederates regard as the "first martyr of the war"?

**A.** James T. Jackson, who killed Ephraim E. Ellsworth and was immediately thereafter killed by one of Ellsworth's men.

---

**Q.** Who improvised the first long-range railway gun, mounted on a railway truck?

**A.** Robert E. Lee, June 1862.

---

**Q.** Where was the first Civil War monument erected?

**A.** Shiloh battleground, late in 1863.

Q. What Confederate is widely believed to have been the first officer killed in battle?

A. Col. Francis S. Bartow, Eighth Georgia, July 21, 1861.

———◆———

Q. What area was included in Department No. 1, C.S.A., in the spring of 1861?

A. Most of Louisiana and parts of Alabama and Mississippi.

---

### "Ladies and Gentlemen, We Present the One and Only . . ."

Only one general officer, Maj. Gen. Sterling Price, often saw his weight drop ten pounds in a single week of fighting—from 300 to 290 pounds.

———◆———

Wealthy Rufus King of New York City was the sole brigadier general on either side to be subject to severe epilepsy. This was compounded by bouts of heavy drinking.

———◆———

One of King's comrades-in-arms, also a brigadier general, reached the Executive Mansion in 1861 and was introduced to President Lincoln as Prince Felix Constantin Alexander Johann Nepomuk Salm-Salm of Prussia. Learning that his royal visitor had a distinguished record and wished to fight for the Union, the president named him a colonel on the spot. Later promoted, he was the only high-ranking officer who did not speak a word of English.

———◆———

German-born William C. Kueffner, who fought under Salm-Salm, never rose above the rank of captain. His meticulous diary showed that he was wounded in less than 4 percent of the 110 engagements in which he fought.

[LIBRARY OF CONGRESS]

*Union commanders did not consider their men ready to fight, but their ninety-day enlistments were about to expire. Goaded into action by Abraham Lincoln, troops moved forward. Many in Washington expected an easy victory and carried picnic lunches with them in their fancy buggies as they drove out to see the fun. Late in the day, panic set in; soldiers of Federal forces practically ran over one another trying to get away. First Bull Run dispelled all ideas that overwhelming industrial and financial power of the Union would bring a quick end to the conflict.*

Q. What was the specific objective of Henry Heth's Confederate division, which made the first major contact with Union forces at Gettysburg?

A. They were looking for shoes for their troops.

———◆———

Q. Because of heavy casualties, before going into battle, Civil War soldiers devised the first "dog tags" of what materials?

A. Names and addresses were handlettered on handkerchiefs or pieces of paper pinned to uniforms.

**Q.** The CSS *Virginia*, the first ironclad warship of the Civil War, was fashioned from the hull and engines of what Union vessel?

**A.** The USS *Merrimack*.

---

**Q.** On April 19, 1861, the first serious bloodshed of the war occurred between what two groups of combatants?

**A.** The Sixth Massachusetts Infantry and civilians, known as the Baltimore Riots.

---

**Q.** How many were killed during the first bloodshed in Baltimore?

**A.** Five soldiers and twelve civilians (probable count).

---

**Q.** Approximately how many casualties resulted from the first major Civil War military engagement at Bull Run?

**A.** Just under 5,000: 2,000 C.S.A. and 3,000 U.S.A.

---

**Q.** What was the first pitched battle west of the Mississippi River?

**A.** Pea Ridge (Elkhorn Tavern), Arkansas, March 7–8, 1862.

---

**Q.** Who is generally considered the winner of the first battle west of the Mississippi?

**A.** Maj. Gen. Samuel R. Curtis, U.S.A., even though he was greatly outnumbered.

---

**Q.** What war-born news service was first to compete with the Associated Press?

**A.** The Independent News Room, Washington.

---

**Q.** What was the first battle lost by Lee as commander of the Army of Northern Virginia?

**A.** Mechanicsville, or Beaver Dam Creek, Virginia, June 26, 1862.

**Q.** What Confederate was the first to ask a Union commander for surrender terms?

**A.** Brig. Gen. Simon Bolivar Buckner, surrendering to Gen. U. S. Grant at Fort Donelson.

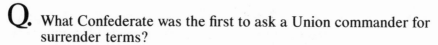

**Q.** What especially colorful troops fought for the C.S.A. in the first battle west of the Mississippi?

**A.** A brigade of Indians led by Albert Pike.

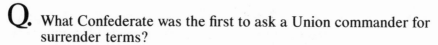

**Q.** What was the first ironclad gunboat of U.S. forces?

**A.** The USS *St. Louis*, launched at Carondelet, Missouri, on October 12, 1861.

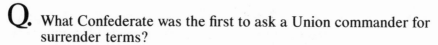

**Q.** Standardized uniforms of Federal units were not required until after what battle?

**A.** In the aftermath of First Bull Run.

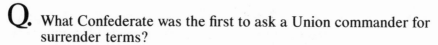

**Q.** Where was blood first spilled west of the Mississippi River?

**A.** St. Louis, May 10, 1861.

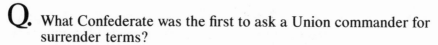

**Q.** Who is generally credited with having won the first engagement of the war?

**A.** Brig. Gen. Daniel H. Hill, C.S.A. (Big Bethel, Virginia, June 1, 1861).

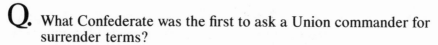

**Q.** What was the first state capital in Confederate territory to be occupied by Union forces?

**A.** Nashville, Tennessee, February 1862.

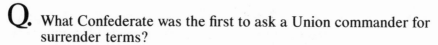

**Q.** Though fought virtually to a draw, what battle did Confederates list as Robert E. Lee's first victory?

**A.** Seven Pines (or Fair Oaks), Virginia, May 31–June 1, 1862.

**Q.** Who was the first (and only) slave trader executed under Federal law?

**A.** Nathaniel Gordon of Portland, Maine (summer 1862).

---

**Q.** What Federal official was the first to go on record as strongly doubting the constitutionality of emancipation by edict?

**A.** Abraham Lincoln.

---

**Q.** Where was some of the first Confederate currency printed?

**A.** New York City, under a contract made before April 1861 and canceled after Fort Sumter.

---

**Q.** From what point was the first shot fired by Union forces at Fort Henry, Tennessee?

**A.** From the gunboat *Cincinnati*, February 6, 1862.

---

**Q.** What underwater vessel was the first to sink a ship in wartime?

**A.** The CSS *H. L. Hunley*, by ramming the USS *Housatonic* in Charleston harbor on February 17, 1864.

---

**Q.** How many troops surrendered at the battle of Fort Donelson, Tennessee?

**A.** More than 12,000.

---

**Q.** Who was the first top official publicly to advocate immediate emancipation and enrollment of black soldiers?

**A.** U.S. secretary of war Simon Cameron in December 1862.

---

**Q.** What was the first significant Union victory in which not a man was lost in combat?

**A.** Capture of Island No. 10, in the Mississippi River, April 7, 1862.

**Q.** What battle was the first to result in almost 25,000 casualties?

**A.** Shiloh, Tennessee (46 percent C.S.A., 54 percent U.S.A.).

———◆———

**Q.** On what occasion did Lincoln first suggest that it might be advisable to issue an emancipation edict?

**A.** En route to the funeral of Edwin M. Stanton's newborn baby, July 1862.

———◆———

**Q.** For the first time since the Thirty Years' War (Germany, 1618–48), what two targets did military strategists, especially Generals Sherman and Sheridan, aim to devastate?

**A.** The enemy's economy and civilian population.

———◆———

**Q.** What Union corps was the first to use two-inch squares of red flannel to identify men of the unit?

**A.** Third Corps, Third Division, in the spring or summer of 1862.

———◆———

**Q.** Where did the first really mammoth use of gunpowder as an explosive take place?

**A.** At Petersburg, Virginia, when 8,000 pounds were detonated at The Crater.

———◆———

**Q.** What branch of the military was in charge of the first Federal gunboats on the Mississippi River?

**A.** The U.S. Army.

———◆———

**Q.** What was the first and only Confederate unit officially to be named for a person?

**A.** The Stonewall Brigade (the First Brigade/Virginia Volunteers), commanded by Stonewall Jackson.

Q. What commanding officer was the first in U.S. history to head an army as large as 30,000 men?

A. Brig. Gen. Irvin McDowell.

---

Q. What vessels were engaged in the first modern naval battle between ironclads?

A. The USS *Monitor* and the CSS *Virginia*, formerly the USS *Merrimac*.

---

Q. Who first defined the term *Lost Cause*, referring to the South's unsuccessful attempt to leave the Union?

A. Journalist Edward A. Pollard in his book *The Lost Cause*, 1866.

---

Q. Who financed the first unofficial medals bestowed upon Union fighting men, the defenders of Fort Sumter?

A. The New York State Chamber of Commerce.

---

Q. What regiment is widely considered to have been first to break and flee at First Bull Run?

A. The First Rhode Island.

---

Q. Who led the first troops attacked by Confederates at Shiloh?

A. Maj. Gen. Benjamin M. Prentiss, Sixth Division.

---

Q. Where did the first—and very rarely used—amphibious landing under enemy fire of troops take place?

A. Roanoke Island, North Carolina, February 8, 1862.

---

Q. What officer of the U.S. Army was the first to reject an offer to become commanding general?

A. Col. Robert E. Lee, who instead joined the Confederate army.

**Q.** What was the first plantation mansion seized by Federal forces?

**A.** Arlington, the property of Mrs. Robert E. Lee.

———◆———

**Q.** Why is the Civil War regarded as the first modern war?

**A.** It was the first total war aiming to destroy the heart of a country, rather than just its army, with new strategy, weapons, and military techniques.

———◆———

**Q.** For the first time in a large-scale war, troops were deployed en masse via what transportation system?

**A.** Railroads.

———◆———

**Q.** Passage of what congressional act on March 3, 1863, was a "first" for the U. S. government?

**A.** The National Conscription Act, as before that the North had relied on volunteers and state militia.

# 6

# Persons, Sites, Actions, and Things

Q. What milk product, patented in 1856, became an important part of the Union soldiers' diets?

A. Gail Borden's condensed milk.

◆

Q. What was the name of Robert E. Lee's beloved horse, now memorialized at Washington and Lee University?

A. Traveller.

◆

Q. What was the name of Jefferson Davis's last home, which after his death became a home for Confederate veterans and their wives or widows and is now a museum?

A. Beauvoir, at Biloxi, Mississippi.

◆

Q. What state university, whose students left en masse in 1861 to join the University Grays or the Lamar Rifles, is best known by its nickname, the antebellum term for the mistress of a southern plantation?

A. Ole Miss, the University of Mississippi.

◆

Q. When the Federal government confiscated Mrs. Robert E. Lee's ancestral mansion where the Lees lived before the war, what use was made of the property?

A. Arlington National Cemetery surrounds Arlington House.

**Q.** What was the standard manual on infantry tactics, used by both armies, which had been written in 1853 at the request of the secretary of war, Jefferson Davis?

**A.** Hardee's *Tactics*, by subsequent Confederate general William J. Hardee.

---

### Men and Mounts

Only one book describes the Civil War as seen through the eyes of a horse: Traveller, Robert E. Lee's favorite mount. Before he became famous as companion to the commander of the Army of Northern Virginia, Traveller was called Jeff Davis and then Greenbrier. Several notable leaders of the war are closely identified with their mounts; some even had two favorites:

Gen. George B. McClellan, *Dan Webster* and *Kentuck*
Gen. "Stonewall" Jackson, *Little Sorrel*
Gen. U. S. Grant, *Cincinnati, Jack, Kangaroo*, and *Fox*
Gen. Nathan Bedford Forrest, *King Phillip*
Gen. Philip Kearny, *Bayard*
Belle Boyd, *Fleeter*
Gen. Albert S. Johnston, *Fire-eater*
Gen. George G. Meade, *Baldy*

---

**Q.** The brilliant tactics of what general were studied in military academies from West Point to St. Cyr in France up to World War I?

**A.** Robert E. Lee.

---◆---

**Q.** As an eighteen-year-old first lieutenant, what future U.S. general earned the Medal of Honor at Missionary Ridge, an award given to his son seventy-nine years later, making them the only father-son combination ever to receive the distinguished medal?

**A.** Arthur MacArthur, Jr., father of Gen. Douglas MacArthur, of World War II fame.

**Q.** Why did their opponents call Northerners who sympathized with the South "copperheads"?

**A.** Some wore copper pennies as identifying badges.

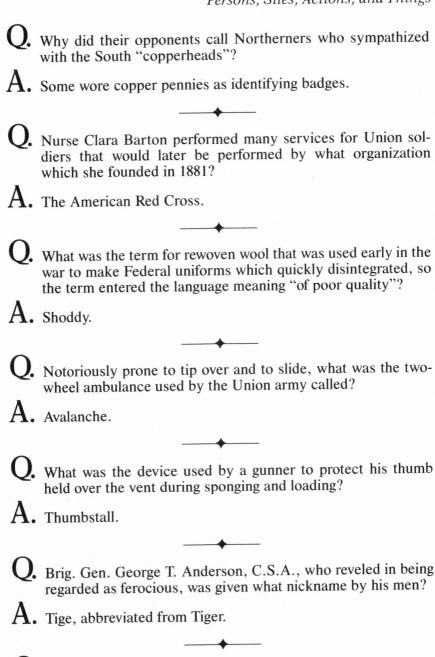

**Q.** Nurse Clara Barton performed many services for Union soldiers that would later be performed by what organization which she founded in 1881?

**A.** The American Red Cross.

**Q.** What was the term for rewoven wool that was used early in the war to make Federal uniforms which quickly disintegrated, so the term entered the language meaning "of poor quality"?

**A.** Shoddy.

**Q.** Notoriously prone to tip over and to slide, what was the two-wheel ambulance used by the Union army called?

**A.** Avalanche.

**Q.** What was the device used by a gunner to protect his thumb held over the vent during sponging and loading?

**A.** Thumbstall.

**Q.** Brig. Gen. George T. Anderson, C.S.A., who reveled in being regarded as ferocious, was given what nickname by his men?

**A.** Tige, abbreviated from Tiger.

**Q.** In what year were conquered banners returned peacefully to the South?

**A.** 1905 (President Grover Cleveland had approved their return in 1887, but indignation among Northerners caused him to revoke the order).

**Q.** By what other name is the battle of Shiloh known?

**A.** The battle of Pittsburg Landing, Tennessee.

———◆———

**Q.** When six movable guns of the same caliber were grouped together, what did they form?

**A.** A field battery.

———◆———

**Q.** What unit was formed by placing three divisions under a single commander?

**A.** A corps.

———◆———

**Q.** What Union general, widely known as Little Napoleon, seemed to revel in the nickname?

**A.** George B. McClellan.

———◆———

**Q.** What was the designation of a mounted sentinel on guard duty in advance of an outpost?

**A.** Vidette.

———◆———

**Q.** What smooth-bore piece of heavy artillery, used by both sides for coastal fortifications, seemed to perpetuate the name of a famous explorer?

**A.** The Columbiad.

———◆———

**Q.** Described as "infernal machines" and used extensively by the Confederates, torpedoes are today called by what name?

**A.** Mines.

———◆———

**Q.** Nicknamed "Unconditional Surrender" Grant after Fort Donelson, the Union general was called by what nickname as a cadet?

**A.** Uncle Sam.

*Some of his subordinates claimed that Gideon Welles of Connecticut had never been aboard a ship until he became Lincoln's secretary of the navy. Many professional fighting men who saw his flowing beard for the first time agreed that it was appropriate to call him Father Neptune. In spite of lacking experience and appearing to be a "benevolent old gentleman," Welles made the U.S. Navy what many regarded as the most efficient fighting force of the Civil War. Unlike four fellow members of the Lincoln cabinet, he never aspired to the presidency. But he often listened when colleagues spoke and preserved in his diary records of many high-level conferences about which we would otherwise know little or nothing.*

[LIBRARY OF CONGRESS]

**Q.** What was the large-bore cannon with a short barrel, strictly for use at close range?

**A.** A carronade.

---

**Q.** When ten companies were grouped under a single commander, what was the larger unit called?

**A.** A regiment.

---

**Q.** The familiar forage cap with a round flat crown and visor worn in both armies was called by what French name?

**A.** Kepi.

**Q.** What was the name of the defensive fortification formed from felled trees, facing outward?

**A.** An abatis.

---

**Q.** Because veteran engineer Robert E. Lee often set men to digging, what was he frequently called?

**A.** King of Spades.

---

**Q.** What jocular name was given to C.S.A. units made up of volunteers from Arkansas and Texas?

**A.** Rackansackers.

---

**Q.** What artillery shot consisted of two iron plates connected by a bolt, with nine or more iron balls between them?

**A.** Grapeshot.

---

**Q.** An officer of what rank usually led five regiments?

**A.** Brigadier general.

---

**Q.** When a battery succeeded in firing upon the length of an enemy body, what was this action called?

**A.** Enfilade.

---

**Q.** What was the name of the two-wheel ammunition chest that was attached to each piece of field artillery?

**A.** A limber.

---

**Q.** When fifty to one hundred men were grouped under a single leader, what was the unit called?

**A.** A company, commanded by a captain.

## Two Lees at West Point Simultaneously

Fitzhugh Lee of Fairfax, Virginia, was overjoyed at news he would enter West Point in 1852. Destined to become a Confederate major general, he had decided upon a military career in early adolescence. Fitzhugh Lee graduated number forty-five in the class of 1856, thankful that he had survived.

His Uncle Robert began a three-year term as superintendent in the year Fitzhugh entered. "Behavior not becoming an officer and a gentleman" brought the cadet into the office of his uncle. Acting as though he had never seen the cadet, Robert E. Lee stopped just short of expelling his nephew.

Q. When inmates of a Petersburg prison heard the constant thunder of big guns, what did they name the place?

A. Castle Thunder.

———◆———

Q. When two or more corps had a single commander, what was the larger unit named?

A. An army, often far below theoretical strength.

———◆———

Q. What special name did Union troops fighting in the South give to diarrhea?

A. The Tennessee quickstep.

———◆———

Q. What name did gunners affectionately bestow on especially big shells, usually those weighing one hundred pounds or more?

A. Lamp posts.

———◆———

Q. After lackluster performance until Petersburg, what regal nickname was given to John B. Magruder, C.S.A?

A. Prince John.

**Q.** Until he was killed in the final days of the war, by what name did subordinates refer to C.S.A. lieutenant general A. P. Hill?

**A.** Little Powell.

———◆———

**Q.** Why was Maj. Gen. Benjamin F. Butler derisively called "Spoons"?

**A.** He was accused of having stolen the family silver from the New Orleans home where he had his headquarters.

———◆———

**Q.** A bombastic order issued by John Pope, Army of Virginia, led to his receiving what derisive nickname?

**A.** Five-Cent Pope.

———◆———

**Q.** When three or more brigades were combined to form a standard tactical unit, what was it called?

**A.** A division, typically headed by a major general.

———◆———

**Q.** During the March to the Sea, what name was given to Sherman's soldiers who were authorized to live off the land?

**A.** Bummers.

———◆———

**Q.** Poorly supplied with uniforms, some Confederate volunteers wore homespun attire dyed a yellowish-brown, from which they derived what nickname?

**A.** Butternuts, which were used to color the cloth.

———◆———

**Q.** Among the six horses that drew a piece of field artillery, what were those closest to the gun called?

**A.** The wheel pair.

[LESLIE'S ILLUSTRATED WEEKLY]

Many officers had favorite horses, whom they named and treated almost like members of the family. There is no record that a single lowly mule was ever identified by name in a military report. Yet the mule was to Civil War units what the Jeep became in the era of mechanized warfare. Pound for pound, practically all mules were stronger than horses. That meant they literally pulled armies from one battlefield to another. Several hundred of them—anonymous, like all the rest—were basic to one of the war's strangest raids. For seventeen days, Col. Abel D. Streight led men mounted on 800 mules through the hills of northern Alabama. Although his "mule brigade" was the talk of the North for a while, it went down in defeat before horseriding cavalrymen of Nathan B. Forrest.

**Q.** One of five Confederate generals killed in the battle of Franklin, Tennessee, what were the unusual but relevant baptismal names of Major General Gist?

**A.** States Rights.

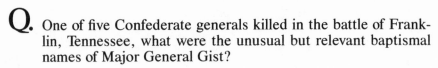

**Q.** Photographic images, 2.5 by 4 inches, which soldiers posed for against standard backgrounds and mailed home to their families, were called by what term?

**A.** Cartes de visite.

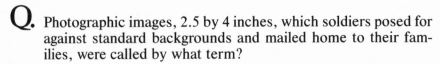

**Q.** A Methodist log meeting house, whose name meant "place of peace," gave its name to what bloody battle?

**A.** Shiloh.

———◆———

**Q.** What name was given to an informally organized body, bigger than a division but smaller than a corps?

**A.** Wing or command, used interchangeably.

———◆———

**Q.** Inspired by the nickname of his cousin Stonewall, by what designation was C.S.A. colonel William L. Jackson known?

**A.** Mudwall.

———◆———

**Q.** When punished by being forced to sit for hours on a fence rail, what did a soldier call his mount?

**A.** The wooden mule.

———◆———

**Q.** What was the name of special details of men who during assaults used bayonet points, if necessary, to keep stragglers in line?

**A.** File closers.

**Q.** What did gunners at Petersburg name the thirteen-inch mortar mounted on a flatcar that pounded Confederate lines?

**A.** The Dictator.

---

**Q.** What nickname expressing admiration was bestowed upon barely literate Nathan B. Forrest, C.S.A.?

**A.** Wizard of the Saddle.

---

**Q.** What was the term fighting men had for the gold braid on an officer's coat?

**A.** Chicken guts.

---

**Q.** One of the four major generals appointed by President Lincoln at the beginning of the war, John Charles Frémont was a national hero who was known by what epithet?

**A.** The Pathfinder, because of his trailblazing of the West.

---

**Q.** What was the designation of a fleet made up of small vessels?

**A.** A flotilla.

---

**Q.** When a fellow lost in casting of lots, what was he likely to be called?

**A.** A short-straw man.

---

**Q.** What document issued to a ship's captain by the C.S.A. authorized "legalized piracy"?

**A.** A letter of marque.

---

**Q.** The skinny legs of Nathan G. Evans, defender of the Stone Bridge at Antietam, inspired what nickname?

**A.** Shanks.

**Q.** Why did the Confederate military dislike the official Stars and Bars flag?

**A.** Its similarity to the U.S. flag caused confusion in battle.

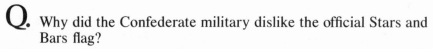

**Q.** By what name was Richard S. Ewell, successor to Stonewall Jackson, called?

**A.** Old Baldy.

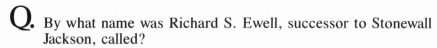

**Q.** Why do many Civil War battles have two names, such as Bull Run/Manassas or Stone's River/Murfreesboro?

**A.** Confederates named battles after the nearest settlement, while Yankees named them after the nearest body of water.

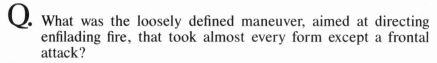

**Q.** By what other name was the battle of Brice's Cross Roads, Mississippi, widely known to those who fought in it?

**A.** The battle of Guntown.

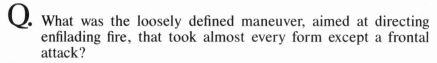

**Q.** What was the loosely defined maneuver, aimed at directing enfilading fire, that took almost every form except a frontal attack?

**A.** The envelopment, used extremely often.

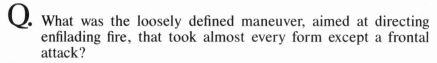

**Q.** What was the small-scale strategic movement executed in an attempt to draw attention away from the real target?

**A.** The feint.

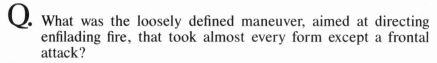

**Q.** What name was given to Walt Disney's movie about Andrews's Raid against the Western and Atlantic Railroad?

**A.** *The Great Locomotive Chase.*

*Prussian-born Carl Schurz worked for the election of Abraham Lincoln and was rewarded by being made U.S. minister to Spain. He chafed in that post, so he resigned and asked for a military commission. Lincoln reluctantly gave it to him, largely as a concession to German citizens in blue uniforms. He fought gallantly but not brilliantly, yet became a major general. Out of uniform for a few months in 1864, he performed his most valuable service to the man he revered by helping underdog Lincoln to win reelection.*

[*DICTIONARY OF AMERICAN PORTRAITS*]

**Q.** What nickname was attached to fiery Maj. Gen. Joseph Hooker, U.S.A.?

**A.** Fighting Joe.

◆

**Q.** Similar to grapeshot, what can-shaped projectile usually contained forty-eight balls rather than nine?

**A.** Canister.

◆

**Q.** When two or more pieces of field artillery moved frequently and rapidly along a battle line, what were they called?

**A.** A flying battery.

◆

**Q.** What poetic-sounding name was given to the battle of Lookout Mountain?

**A.** Battle above the Clouds.

**Q.** When the war began, to whom did Abraham Lincoln offer the field command of the armies of the United States?

**A.** Robert E. Lee, a colonel in the U.S. Army.

———◆———

**Q.** By what other name is the battle of Antietam widely known?

**A.** The battle of Sharpsburg.

———◆———

**Q.** What famous detective agency was founded by the man selected to organize the U.S. Secret Service during the war?

**A.** Pinkerton Detective Agency.

———◆———

**Q.** What was a small, often temporary, defensive earthwork or breastwork called?

**A.** A redoubt.

———◆———

**Q.** Charging infantry were stopped by what barrier made of trimmed trees or timbers fitted with long stakes, pointed outward?

**A.** Chevaux-de-frise.

———◆———

**Q.** What early Union invader of Virginia issued proclamations saying he did not intend to interfere with slavery?

**A.** George B. McClellan, Army of the Potomac.

———◆———

**Q.** By what name were Lincoln's most vocal Northern opponents—abolitionists of his own party—known?

**A.** Black Republicans.

———◆———

**Q.** What refugee recruited Americans of German descent for the Union and wrote letters of advice to Lincoln?

**A.** Carl Schurz, minister to Spain, then major general.

## West Pointers

U.S. Grant and James Longstreet spent three years together at West Point before going separate ways upon the war's outbreak.

＋

After Kirby Smith parted company with his classmate George Morgan, the two did not see one another again until they met at Cumberland Gap, on opposite sides.

＋

Robert Anderson taught P. T. G. Beauregard artillery, only to have the guns of his former student turned upon him at Fort Sumter.

＋

P. T. G. Beauregard was second in the class of 1838, and his classmate and future foe at First Bull Run, Irvin McDowell, was twenty-third among the forty-five graduates.

＋

Because George B. McClellan was second in the class of 1846, he tended to look down his nose at comparatively low-ranking Thomas J. Jackson, seventeenth of fifty-nine graduates and years away from becoming known as Stonewall.

＋

Ambrose E. Burnside (1847), John G. Foster (1848), John G. Parke (1849), and Jesse L. Reno (1846) did not spend a lot of time together when all were at West Point. But when each man played a part in the expedition against Roanoke Island in February 1862, their subordinates dubbed them the Four Horsemen of the Point.

Q. What leader of the Army of the Potomac kept a personal bodyguard on duty much of the time?

A. George B. McClellan.

◆

Q. When the engineer of a military locomotive got the signal "full speed ahead," what did he call it?

A. The highball.

◆

Q. To what name was the Army of the Ohio changed by presidential directive?

A. The Army of the Cumberland.

---

### Civil War Artists

Henry Love, only newspaper artist at Shiloh.
Theodore R. Davis, *Harper's Weekly*.
Winslow Homer, later one of the nation's best-loved painters.
Alfred R. Waud, a native of Britain who was called "Wode."
William Waud, older brother of Alfred.
Edwin Forbes, *Leslie's Illustrated Weekly*.
Charles W. Reed, in the thick of the fighting at Gettysburg.
Thomas Nast, who helped overthrow New York's Tweed ring.
James Walker, English painter at Lookout Mountain.
William L. Shepherd, a Confederate soldier.
John Adams Elder, famous for painting Petersburg's Battle of The Crater.
Frank Vizetelly, sketch artist for the *Illustrated London News*.
Conrad Wise Chapman, wounded at Shiloh.
William L. Sheppard (of the C.S.A.), artist for *Battles and Leaders of the Civil War*.
Alan C. Redwood, another Confederate who helped illustrate *Battles and Leaders of the Civil War*.
Adalbert J. Volck, a Baltimore dentist-turned-sketch-artist who turned out caricatures of Abraham Lincoln.

---

*Artists who depicted Nathan Bedford Forrest confessed that they never quite managed to capture the entity of the Wizard of the Saddle. Of all who fought, only he enlisted as a private and rose to the rank of major general before war's end. A semiliterate son of a blacksmith, he became a self-made millionaire who led his scruffy looking men to victory after victory. One of his long-time opponents, Gen. William T. Sherman, called the Confederate cavalryman the "most remarkable man our Civil War produced on either side."*

**Q.** What mocking name was given to 25,000 untrained volunteers who fought under George P. Buell, U.S.A.?

**A.** Squirrel Hunters.

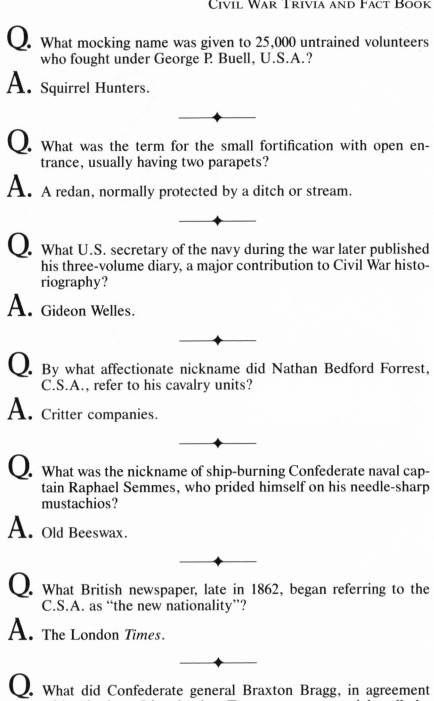

**Q.** What was the term for the small fortification with open entrance, usually having two parapets?

**A.** A redan, normally protected by a ditch or stream.

**Q.** What U.S. secretary of the navy during the war later published his three-volume diary, a major contribution to Civil War historiography?

**A.** Gideon Welles.

**Q.** By what affectionate nickname did Nathan Bedford Forrest, C.S.A., refer to his cavalry units?

**A.** Critter companies.

**Q.** What was the nickname of ship-burning Confederate naval captain Raphael Semmes, who prided himself on his needle-sharp mustachios?

**A.** Old Beeswax.

**Q.** What British newspaper, late in 1862, began referring to the C.S.A. as "the new nationality"?

**A.** The London *Times*.

**Q.** What did Confederate general Braxton Bragg, in agreement with Abraham Lincoln that Tennessee was crucial, call the state?

**A.** The Shield of the South.

**Q.** What names were given to small Confederate ships whose skippers tried to shield them with bales of cotton?

**A.** Cotton clads.

---

**Q.** What were men of some units called who specialized in rapidly laying down pontoon bridges for Union forces?

**A.** Pontoniers.

---

**Q.** Some Federal warships, used on inland waters and protected by thin coats of iron, were commonly called by what name?

**A.** Tinclads.

---

**Q.** When Union troops didn't call their foes Rebels, Butternuts, or Johnnies, what name might they use?

**A.** Graybacks.

---

**Q.** When Kirby Smith, C.S.A., organized the Department of West Louisiana and Texas, what name did it take?

**A.** Kirby-Smithdom.

---

**Q.** By what name did soldiers on leave in Washington often designate faded and aging prostitutes?

**A.** Dead rabbits.

---

**Q.** What was the name of the "world's largest hospital" in Richmond, containing 150 buildings?

**A.** Chimborazo, for the Chimborazo Heights.

---

**Q.** What nickname was given to Confederate bills of small denominations?

**A.** Shinplasters.

Q. What affectionate name was given to whiskey whose Richmond price soared to thirty-five dollars a gallon?

A. Bust-head, tangle-foot, or red-eye.

＋

Q. What Tennessee railroad town, briefly headquarters for Braxton Bragg, C.S.A., bore an Indian name meaning "mud"?

A. Tullahoma.

＋

Q. When Unionists of the deep South joined the ranks of fighting men in blue, what were they commonly called?

A. Homemade Yankees.

＋

Q. Bleedings, dosages of opium or quinine, and application of mustard plasters were the ways of treating what prevalent kind of illness among soldiers?

A. Respiratory diseases such as pneumonia or bronchitis.

＋

Q. What was the full name of the handsome and dashing Ohio native, number one in his West Point class of 1853, who died at Atlanta?

A. Maj. Gen. James Birdseye McPherson.

＋

Q. Engineers who specialized in digging fortifications were given what special name?

A. Sappers (from *sap*, meaning "fortification").

＋

Q. Where did the September 1864 siege of Fort Gibson take place?

A. Indian Territory.

Q. What was the most common name for C.S.A. fighters, still civilians, who raided, burned, and plundered in enemy territory?

A. Partisan Rangers.

Q. Blinded Brig. Gen. Adam R. Johnson, C.S.A., had what nickname?

A. Stovepipe.

Q. What did engineers call a wicker basket, filled with earth and stones, used to reinforce fieldworks?

A. A gabion.

Q. What nickname was given to Brig. Gen. Martin W. Gary, C.S.A., whose command was the last to leave Richmond?

A. The Bald Eagle.

Q. After men under Col. Charles R. Jennison, U.S.A., depopulated three Kansas counties, what was the region called?

A. The Burnt District.

Q. Privately owned vessels authorized by the C.S.A. to prey upon Union shipping were called by what name?

A. Privateers.

Q. Northerners who came to the South after the war for political or financial gain were called what name by former Confederates?

A. Carpetbaggers.

## Numbers May Not Be Everything, But . . .

During a five-minute period beginning about 4:30 P.M. on August 30, 1862, men of Col. Gouverneur Warren's Fifth New York Regiment tried to stem the gray tide launched by James Longstreet. During five minutes, 61 percent of the Union force became casualties. No other infantry regiment lost so many men during such a brief interval.

———◆———

John Singleton Mosby of Virginia wanted to fight for the Confederacy, but not as a member of an existing army. For weeks, he badgered commanders for permission to organize his own band under the Partisan Ranger Law. Finally given permission, Mosby started his Forty-third Battalion, Virginia Cavalry, with just eight followers. Robert E. Lee's papers refer to Mosby more often than to any other Confederate leader. At one time or another, an estimated 1,900 men fought under this partisan—seldom more than 800 at a time—and by his estimate he succeeded in immobilizing at least 30,000 men in blue.

———◆———

Because Kentucky remained in the Union, 1,512 citizens who volunteered for Confederate service went into the Orphan Brigade. Before this body of valiant warriors surrendered on May 6, 1865, at Washington, Georgia, its members recorded 1,860 deaths and serious wounds, against less than one dozen desertions.

Q. What military term means "the art of maneuvering troops in order to achieve victory in combat"?

A. Tactics.

———◆———

Q. What cylindrical pivots permit a cannon or mortar to be elevated and lowered quickly?

A. Trunnions.

Q. What affectionate nickname was given to Jubal A. Early, C.S.A., by his men?

A. Old Jube.

———————◆———————

Q. What name was given to the day on which Robert E. Lee's retreating men were overwhelmed, April 6, 1865?

A. Black Thursday.

———————◆———————

Q. Following surrender, white southern Republicans, regarded as traitorous by their fellow citizens, were given what opprobrious title?

A. Scalawags.

# 7

# Numbers Tell Their Own Stories

**Q.** In the election of 1860, what percentage of the voters backed Abraham Lincoln, who had pledged to preserve the Union, whatever the cost?

**A.** Just under 40 percent.

———◆———

**Q.** What was the population of the United States in 1860, slaves included, but American Indians not counted?

**A.** 31,443,321.

———◆———

**Q.** During 1861–65, with more than 955,000 immigrants arriving, what was the approximate division to the North and South?

**A.** 764,000 to the North, 191,000 to the South.

———◆———

**Q.** At Antietam, or Sharpsburg, about how many casualties were suffered on Wednesday, September 17, 1862?

**A.** 26,000: 13,700 C.S.A.; 12,400 U.S.A.

———◆———

**Q.** How many men were in the Pennsylvania units that reached Washington on April 18, 1861, constituting its only important defense?

**A.** About 500, five companies.

*Had anyone other than Abraham Lincoln gone to the White House in 1860, there is no certainty the Civil War would have erupted. Only the man from Illinois was so wedded to the notion of the perpetual Union that he refused to consider a compromise of any sort. In 1860 no women voted; neither did any slaves. That meant the electorate was comprised almost entirely of white males who had paid taxes or served in the military. Out of the total population of the nation at the time, one person in seventeen voted for Lincoln, enough to put him where he could make decisions that led to war of brother against brother.*

[C. S. GERMAN PHOTO, NATIONAL ARCHIVES]

Q. Of the 30,500 miles of railroads in the country in 1860, what percentage lay in Confederate territory?

A. 28 percent.

------◆------

Q. The two warring capitals—Washington, D.C., and Richmond, Virginia—are how far apart?

A. About one hundred miles.

------◆------

Q. How many states had announced their secession from the Union at the time Abraham Lincoln was inaugurated?

A. Seven (South Carolina, Mississippi, Florida, Alabama, Georgia, Louisiana, and Texas).

**Q.** Of the 128,000 manufacturing establishments in the United States in 1860, what percentage were in the North?

**A.** 86 percent.

---

**Q.** What percentage of the population of the Confederacy were slaves?

**A.** 38 percent.

---

**Q.** Free blacks comprised what percentage of the population of the northern states?

**A.** 1 percent.

---

**Q.** In the wake of the United States's seizure of C.S.A. commissioners from the ship *Trent*, Britain dispatched how many troops to Canada?

**A.** Eight thousand.

---

**Q.** How many states seceded to form the Confederacy?

**A.** Eleven.

---

**Q.** According to the prisoner exchange agreement of July 1862, how many privates would be exchanged for one general?

**A.** Sixty.

---

**Q.** How many bridges spanned the Potomac River, linking Washington with Alexandria, Virginia?

**A.** Two.

---

**Q.** How many dollars did a northern newspaper offer for the capture of C.S.A. major general Earl Van Dorn?

**A.** Five thousand.

**Q.** What was the most common of all camp maladies, which accounted for the deaths of more than 44,000 U.S. soldiers?

**A.** Diarrhea, including dysentery.

---

**Q.** How many guns were carried by the ironclad vessel, the *Monitor*?

**A.** Two (eleven-inch Dahlgren smoothbores).

---

**Q.** In millions, what was the U.S. national debt in 1860?

**A.** $64.8.

---

**Q.** In billions, what was the U.S. national debt at the close of the war in 1865?

**A.** $2.7 (an increase of 4,100 percent).

---

**Q.** How many dollars did the U.S. spend for veterans' compensation and pensions in 1860?

**A.** $1,103 per veteran.

---

**Q.** What percentage of the nation's factory workers were in the North in 1860?

**A.** 92 percent, out of a total of 1.4 million workers.

---

**Q.** When a major general took over a military post or fort, how many guns were fired as a salute to him?

**A.** Forty.

---

**Q.** The largest amphibious expedition to date was assembled in 1862 to transport McClellan's forces to what campaign?

**A.** The Peninsula.

**Q.** How many American Revolutions could have been financed for the estimated cost of the Civil War?

**A.** More than sixty-eight ($12.5 billion as compared to $190 million).

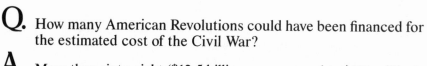

**Q.** During the course of the conflict, how many men were enlisted in all branches of the Union forces?

**A.** 2,778,304.

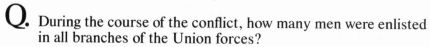

**Q.** What was the total C.S.A. enlistment for the war years?

**A.** The exact number is unknown, perhaps as many as 1,400,000 or as few as 600,000, depending on the authority's estimates.

---

**Q.** In states loyal to the Union, how many males were drafted and classified for military service?

**A.** 777,000.

---

**Q.** How many males were drafted and classified for military service in the C.S.A.?

**A.** No one knows (many records, sparse from the beginning, were destroyed and cannot be reconstructed).

---

**Q.** How did Island No. 10, a site of major strategical importance, get its unusual name?

**A.** Starting at the mouth of the Ohio River and going south, it was the tenth island in the Mississippi River.

---

**Q.** During the Easter season of 1862, approximately how many pounds of iron were thrown by naval guns against Confederates defending New Orleans?

**A.** 3,400,000.

**Q.** What is the estimated ratio, Union to Confederate, of men potentially available for military service in 1861?

**A.** 3.5:1.

———◆———

**Q.** How many states were classified as "border states," remaining in the Union but with strong ties to the South?

**A.** Four: Delaware, Maryland, Kentucky, and Missouri.

———◆———

**Q.** Of the 75,000 residents of the District of Columbia in 1860, how many were black, and of these, how many were slaves?

**A.** 14,000 blacks, 3,000 slaves.

---

### Someone Had to Do It

Throughout the war, Union armies operated under a system of geographical departments. This arrangement was created by John C. Calhoun of nullification and secession fame, then modified by U.S. secretary of war Jefferson Davis. The Calhoun-Davis plan saw few alterations of consequence during the four years it functioned against the C.S.A.

When the Great Seal of the Confederacy was designed, a decision was reached to place a horseman in its center. That rider was the Father of His Country, George Washington.

---

**Q.** When Henry W. Halleck became commander in chief of Union forces in July 1862, what was remarkable about their size?

**A.** At 120,000 men, the Union army was the largest assembled in the Western hemisphere to date.

———◆———

**Q.** What was the largest city in the Confederacy, with a population of 168,000 in 1860?

**A.** New Orleans.

**Q.** With a population exceeding 800,000 in 1860, what was the largest city in the North?

**A.** New York.

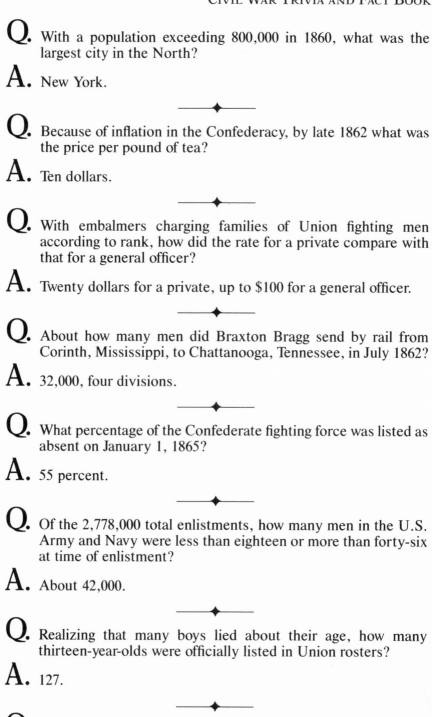

**Q.** Because of inflation in the Confederacy, by late 1862 what was the price per pound of tea?

**A.** Ten dollars.

**Q.** With embalmers charging families of Union fighting men according to rank, how did the rate for a private compare with that for a general officer?

**A.** Twenty dollars for a private, up to $100 for a general officer.

**Q.** About how many men did Braxton Bragg send by rail from Corinth, Mississippi, to Chattanooga, Tennessee, in July 1862?

**A.** 32,000, four divisions.

**Q.** What percentage of the Confederate fighting force was listed as absent on January 1, 1865?

**A.** 55 percent.

**Q.** Of the 2,778,000 total enlistments, how many men in the U.S. Army and Navy were less than eighteen or more than forty-six at time of enlistment?

**A.** About 42,000.

**Q.** Realizing that many boys lied about their age, how many thirteen-year-olds were officially listed in Union rosters?

**A.** 127.

**Q.** What was the height of Capt. Van Buskird of the Twenty-seventh Indiana, tallest man in the Union forces?

**A.** Six feet, ten and one-half inches.

———◆———

**Q.** What was the height of the shortest man in the Union forces?

**A.** Three feet, four inches (a private in the 192nd Ohio).

———◆———

**Q.** About how many railroad cars were needed to move a 10,000-man mixed division, infantry and artillery?

**A.** At least 270 boxcars.

———◆———

**Q.** How many states were in the Union in 1860?

**A.** Thirty-three.

———◆———

**Q.** How old was John Lincoln ("Johnny") Clem, the Drummer Boy of Chickamauga, when he first tried to enlist?

**A.** Nine years old.

———◆———

**Q.** In 1861, what was a Union soldier's monthly pay?

**A.** Thirteen dollars.

———◆———

**Q.** As president of the United States, what was Abraham Lincoln's annual salary?

**A.** $25,000.

———◆———

**Q.** How many old soldiers attended the last reunion of the United Confederate Veterans in 1951?

**A.** Three.

———◆———

**Q.** Of the 583 general officers in the Union Army, how many died in battle or suffered mortal wounds?

**A.** Forty-seven, or 8 percent of the total number.

Q. Of the 425 Confederate general officers, how many were killed or died from wounds?

A. Seventy-seven, or 18 percent of the total number.

———◆———

Q. Which of the 2,499 Union regiments had the highest death toll?

A. The Fifth New Hampshire, with 295 of its men dead.

———◆———

Q. After the battle of Franklin, Tennessee, how many dead Confederate generals were laid on the back porch of the Carnton House?

A. Five.

———◆———

Q. In the three-day carnage at Gettysburg, what was the combined casualty total of dead, wounded, and missing for the two armies?

A. 51,112.

———◆———

Q. Records suggest that among Confederates, what military unit suffered the most casualties?

A. The Twenty-sixth North Carolina, with 708 out of 880, at Gettysburg alone.

———◆———

Q. With budget receipts of $56,065,000 in 1860, what was the United States deficit for the year?

A. $7,066,000.

———◆———

Q. With budget receipts of $333,715,000 in 1865, what was the United States deficit in 1865?

A. $963,841,000.

[HARPER'S WEEKLY]

A seldom emphasized but major factor contributing to the 12,912 graves at Andersonville prison was U.S. Grant's decision to stop exchanging prisoners. He reasoned that since enlistments of many prisoners were about to expire, why swap a rebel who'd fight to the end for a fellow about ready to go home? Furthermore, the North had abundant manpower, while the supply in the South was dwindling fast. No longer able to get prisoners off their hands, Confederates herded them into Andersonville. The flag-raising ceremony (center rear) featured the presence of Clara Barton, who tried to prevent Union authorities from hanging commandant Henry Wirz as the only "war criminal" of the conflict.

Q. With cotton considered the most important economic bargaining chip of the C.S.A., what was its 1865 production?

A. 2,094,000 bales (54 percent of the 1860 level).

**Q.** When did the last member of the Grand Army of the Republic die?

**A.** 1956, Albert Woolson of Minnesota, a former drummer boy.

---

**Q.** How many blockade runners commanded by Confederate naval officers were captured during the war?

**A.** None.

---

**Q.** How many blacks eventually served in the Union army and navy?

**A.** Almost 200,000.

---

**Q.** Of every one hundred men who served in the U.S. Navy, about how many were free blacks or ex-slaves?

**A.** Twenty-five.

---

**Q.** What Union regiment suffered the largest percentage of one-battle casualties?

**A.** The First Minnesota, 82 percent at Gettysburg.

---

**Q.** Approximately how many cubic feet of gas was held by the largest of Thaddeus Lowe's observation balloons?

**A.** 32,000.

---

**Q.** By the end of the war, how many graves had been dug and filled at the infamous Andersonville Prison?

**A.** 12,912 (total deaths were probably much higher).

---

**Q.** During the Antietam campaign, when Harpers Ferry fell to Stonewall Jackson, how many weapons did he seize?

**A.** Seventy-three cannon and 13,000 small arms (along with 10,000 men).

**Q.** How many horses were needed to pull the six guns of a standard field battery?

**A.** Thirty-six, three pairs in tandem per gun.

———◆———

**Q.** What two-mile-long factory did Col. George W. Rains build to supply materiel for the Confederacy?

**A.** The Augusta (Georgia) Powder Works.

———◆———

**Q.** How many officers and men were in the U.S. Army when Confederates captured Fort Sumter?

**A.** 1,108 officers, 15,259 enlisted men.

———◆———

**Q.** What did it cost Great Britain when an international tribunal settled claims arising from depredations of Confederate cruisers built in the island kingdom?

**A.** $15,500,000, in gold.

———◆———

**Q.** Immediately after Fort Sumter fell to Confederates, Abraham Lincoln called for how many volunteers?

**A.** 75,000.

———◆———

**Q.** How many Confederate generals were killed at Gettysburg?

**A.** Six.

———◆———

**Q.** What did it cost a citizen of the C.S.A. to avoid military service by means of commutation?

**A.** Five hundred dollars.

———◆———

**Q.** In approximately how many battles and skirmishes did black troops participate?

**A.** 450.

**Q.** What was the most popular handgun used by the U.S. Army and Navy, with about 200,000 having been manufactured 1860–72?

**A.** Colt Army and Navy revolvers.

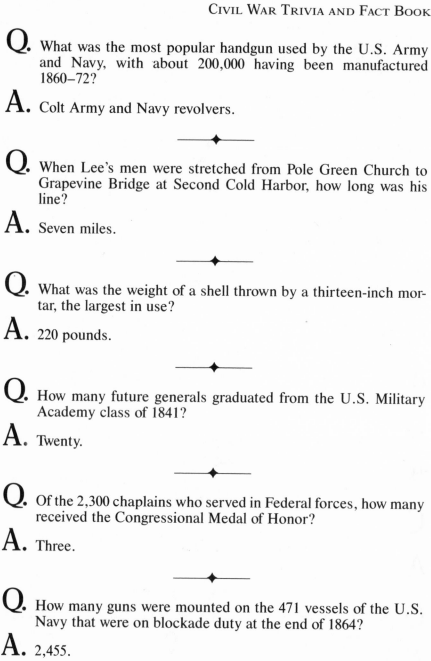

**Q.** When Lee's men were stretched from Pole Green Church to Grapevine Bridge at Second Cold Harbor, how long was his line?

**A.** Seven miles.

**Q.** What was the weight of a shell thrown by a thirteen-inch mortar, the largest in use?

**A.** 220 pounds.

**Q.** How many future generals graduated from the U.S. Military Academy class of 1841?

**A.** Twenty.

**Q.** Of the 2,300 chaplains who served in Federal forces, how many received the Congressional Medal of Honor?

**A.** Three.

**Q.** How many guns were mounted on the 471 vessels of the U.S. Navy that were on blockade duty at the end of 1864?

**A.** 2,455.

**Q.** With the South depending upon cotton to help win the war, what was the value of its farm land in 1860?

**A.** $1,871,000,000.

**Q.** Horses being essential to the war, how many were held in the North and in the South at the start of hostilities?

**A.** North: 4,400,000; South: 1,700,000.

---

**Q.** At Chancellorsville, Virginia, where Stonewall Jackson was mortally wounded, what were total losses of the combatants?

**A.** Hooker lost more than 17,200; Lee lost 12,700.

---

**Q.** The marching ration of a Union soldier consisted of how much bread in addition to meat, sugar, coffee, and salt?

**A.** One pound of hard bread.

---

**Q.** At least three hundred of what special auxiliary troops tried to help defend Fort Fisher, North Carolina?

**A.** Junior Reserves.

---

**Q.** How many big guns did the USS *Carondelet* mount when launched in October 1861?

**A.** Thirteen, one for each port.

---

**Q.** At Gettysburg, how many Confederates were involved in Pickett's charge that was stopped by rifle and artillery fire?

**A.** Fifteen thousand.

---

**Q.** In his October 1862 ride around McClellan's army, how many miles did J. E. B. Stuart and his men traverse in two days?

**A.** More than one hundred.

---

**Q.** Out of every one hundred Union draftees, how many actually served?

**A.** Twenty.

[LESLIE'S ILLUSTRATED WEEKLY]

*Union forces, led by Gen. George B. McClellan (depicted here as just ahead of his color bearer), called the place Antietam from the creek that flows through the region near Sharpsburg, Maryland. It was here that the bloodiest single day of the war saw more than 26,000 casualties in a drawn battle that led Gen. Robert E. Lee to recross the Potomac. Abraham Lincoln regarded the no-win conflict as a sign from heaven, and immediately afterward he made public his preliminary Emancipation Proclamation.*

**Q.** The pacifist Shakers at Pleasant Hill, Kentucky, reported at the end of the war having fed how many soldiers from both armies?

**A.** At least 50,000.

———◆———

**Q.** How many men deserted from Union forces during a typical week in 1863–65?

**A.** 1,250.

**Q.** What was the cost of the war to the Union, not including pensions and interest, as finally tabulated fourteen years after hostilities ceased?

**A.** $6,190,000,000.

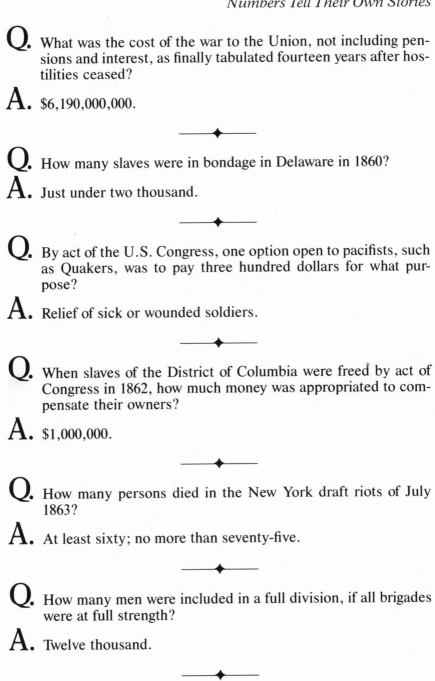

**Q.** How many slaves were in bondage in Delaware in 1860?

**A.** Just under two thousand.

---

**Q.** By act of the U.S. Congress, one option open to pacifists, such as Quakers, was to pay three hundred dollars for what purpose?

**A.** Relief of sick or wounded soldiers.

---

**Q.** When slaves of the District of Columbia were freed by act of Congress in 1862, how much money was appropriated to compensate their owners?

**A.** $1,000,000.

---

**Q.** How many persons died in the New York draft riots of July 1863?

**A.** At least sixty; no more than seventy-five.

---

**Q.** How many men were included in a full division, if all brigades were at full strength?

**A.** Twelve thousand.

---

**Q.** When Confederate raiders descended upon St. Albans, Vermont, how much loot did they get from the banks of the town?

**A.** $200,000.

**Q.** At First Bull Run in July 1861, the best reported of battles, how many newspaper correspondents were present?

**A.** Seventy-six or more (twenty-six from the South, fifty from the North).

———◆———

**Q.** The *Official Records* of both the army and of the navy, begun in 1882 and completed in 1927, contain how many volumes?

**A.** 158.

———◆———

**Q.** What was unusual about the attire of Jubal Early's 14,000 Confederates when they started for Washington in June 1864?

**A.** Half of them were barefoot.

———◆———

**Q.** According to Hardee's *Tactics*, how many thirty-three-inch steps should a soldier take per minute?

**A.** 180.

———◆———

**Q.** How many members of the Fifth Ohio Light Artillery, mustered into service in September 1861 and active until July 1865, died in combat?

**A.** Five.

———◆———

**Q.** How many Confederates died at the Federal prison in Elmira, New York?

**A.** 2,917.

———◆———

**Q.** How many paper dollars, not backed by gold or silver, were printed in Washington during the war?

**A.** 450,000,000.

**Q.** How many of the 106 C.S.A. congressmen were openly "anti-administration" in May 1864?

**A.** Forty-one.

---

**Q.** After Virginia, what state was the site of the most battles?

**A.** Tennessee.

---

**Q.** With the C.S.A. having twenty-six senators, how many won seats in 1864 through opposition to Jefferson Davis?

**A.** Twelve.

---

**Q.** When the C.S.A. Congress authorized recruitment of volunteers in May 1861, how many were wanted?

**A.** 100,000, for six- and twelve-month enlistments.

---

**Q.** How many men were lost in the comparatively obscure battle of Franklin, Tennessee, on November 30, 1864?

**A.** Confederate: more than 6,000; Union: more than 2,000.

---

**Q.** At Cold Harbor, how many Federals died in less than ten minutes?

**A.** At least 6,800.

---

**Q.** When Longstreet moved his army to reinforce Chickamauga—12,000 men a distance of 925 miles—it was accomplished by rail in how many days?

**A.** Eight.

---

**Q.** Each of the six barrels of the Gatling gun could fire how many rounds per minute?

**A.** One hundred.

**Q.** How many dollars did the federal government appropriate to build the USS *Monitor?*

**A.** $275,000.

---

**Q.** How many guns were mounted on the USS *Monitor?*

**A.** Two, on a revolving turret.

---

**Q.** What was the estimated damage done to Georgia during Sherman's ninety-day March to the Sea?

**A.** $100,000,000.

---

**Q.** When its membership peaked in 1890, how many veterans belonged to the Grand Army of the Republic (GAR)?

**A.** 427,981.

---

**Q.** About how many of Sherman's men marched in the August 18, 1865, Grand Review in Washington?

**A.** 65,000.

---

**Q.** What number is attached to the wealthy abolitionists who funneled financial support to John Brown?

**A.** The Secret Six.

---

**Q.** What volume is widely considered to be the standard source of statistical information about the Union and Confederate armies?

**A.** *Numbers and Losses in the Civil War in America, 1861–65*, by Thomas L. Livermore, published in 1900.

---

**Q.** How many ironclad vessels did the C.S.A. put into operation?

**A.** Twenty-two.

**Q.** What is the only state that has compiled a definitive listing of its citizens who served in the war?

**A.** North Carolina.

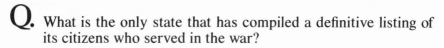

**Q.** For about how many yards did the retreating C.S.A. wagon train stretch after Gettysburg?

**A.** More than 29,900.

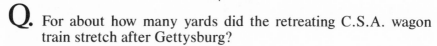

**Q.** Approximately how many prisoners were captured by Federal forces during the course of the conflict?

**A.** At least 215,000.

**Q.** What is the comparable figure for the C.S.A.?

**A.** 205,000.

**Q.** The "Fighting McCooks," an Ohio family, contributed how many of its members to the war?

**A.** Fourteen, including seven sons of Daniel McCook along with seven of their cousins.

**Q.** How many prisoners of war are estimated to have died in captivity?

**A.** Federal: 23,000; Confederate: more than 26,000.

**Q.** How many soldiers and sailors did tiny Rhode Island provide?

**A.** More than 23,000, about 20 percent above its quota.

**Q.** What record number of Confederate prisoners were taken at Sayler's Creek, Virginia, April 6, 1865?

**A.** About 8,000.

## Sometimes Money Does Matter

Transportation magnate Cornelius Vanderbilt prized each of his ships. But as a patriotic gesture, he agreed to sell a 1,700-ton vessel that bore his name to the Federal government—at his own price. He asked for, and received, exactly one dollar.

◆

Rapidly taking steps toward forming the Confederate States of America, secessionists realized early in 1861 that they would need special currency. Early in March they placed an order for the printing of $1 million in paper money. Turned out on schedule, this job was completed—not in Montgomery or in Richmond—but in New York City.

◆

With men willing to enlist as substitutes demanding no less than $500 and as much more as they could get, Richard D. B. Taylor of Athens, Georgia, was desperate to stay out of uniform. Under terms of an 1863 contract, he managed to get John M. Cape to substitute for him in Company A of the Twenty-fourth Regiment of Georgia Volunteers for a mere $3,000 in cash.

◆

Crew members of U.S. Navy vessels split prize money awarded for the capture of enemy ships. When the CSS *Atlanta* brought $300,000, a ten-year-old powder monkey received $176.16. After another capture, however, an adult seaman was rewarded for his bravery by payment of just sixteen cents.

Q. When elevated five degrees, what was the approximate range of the deadly Napoleon field gun?

A. A little more than 1,600 yards.

◆

Q. What was the overall inflation rate of the C.S.A.?

A. 6,000 percent.

—164—

**Q.** How many stars were in the flag Confederate troops carried into battle?

**A.** Thirteen, representing each seceded state and the secession governments of Kentucky and Missouri.

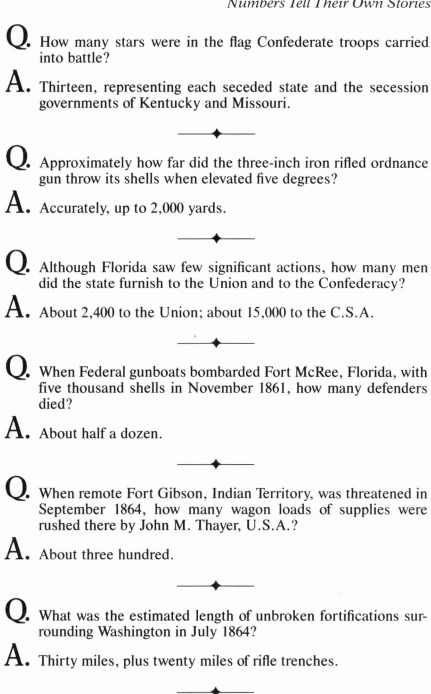

**Q.** Approximately how far did the three-inch iron rifled ordnance gun throw its shells when elevated five degrees?

**A.** Accurately, up to 2,000 yards.

**Q.** Although Florida saw few significant actions, how many men did the state furnish to the Union and to the Confederacy?

**A.** About 2,400 to the Union; about 15,000 to the C.S.A.

**Q.** When Federal gunboats bombarded Fort McRee, Florida, with five thousand shells in November 1861, how many defenders died?

**A.** About half a dozen.

**Q.** When remote Fort Gibson, Indian Territory, was threatened in September 1864, how many wagon loads of supplies were rushed there by John M. Thayer, U.S.A.?

**A.** About three hundred.

**Q.** What was the estimated length of unbroken fortifications surrounding Washington in July 1864?

**A.** Thirty miles, plus twenty miles of rifle trenches.

**Q.** How many military engagements occurred during the war?

**A.** 10,455.

**Q.** To what do the following ratios refer: Federal, 110,100:224,580; Confederate, 94,000:164,000?

**A.** The numbers killed or mortally wounded in battle (first figure) compared to deaths by disease (second figure).

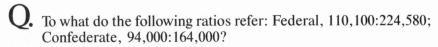

**Q.** While the U.S. government paid pensions and other veterans' benefits to former Federal soldiers, who paid those to Confederate veterans?

**A.** Southern states and private philanthropy.

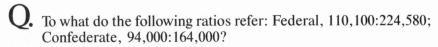

**Q.** The inflation rate was so high that eventually how many Confederate dollars were needed to equal one gold dollar?

**A.** Sixty to seventy.

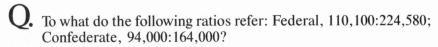

**Q.** At what rate was annual U.S. income taxed in 1862?

**A.** 3 percent for incomes of $600 to $10,000; 5 percent for higher incomes.

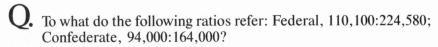

**Q.** Resulting from the war, what was the most serious international problem facing the Grant administration in 1868?

**A.** U.S. claims against Great Britain for shipping losses by Confederate cruisers built and outfitted in England.

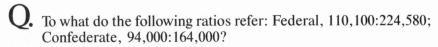

**Q.** What Confederate ship cruised the South Atlantic for twenty-one months, over 75,000 miles of ocean, refueling in foreign ports, and returned with prizes worth over $6.5 million?

**A.** The CSS *Alabama*.

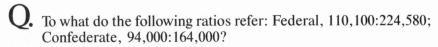

**Q.** After Second Bull Run, for how long did some wounded remain unattended on the battlefield because of inadequacies of the ambulance service?

**A.** Up to one week.

*Hard-hitting C.S.A. general Jubal Early was not the only commander who sometimes had no shoes for his men. As a matter of fact, the location of one of the decisive battles of the war—Gettysburg—was a matter of chance. Troops wandering into the village because a supply of shoes was said to be on hand chanced there to meet the enemy. Within hours the mightiest conflict on North American soil was under way— fought by about 150,000 men— most or all of whom had shoes.*

[NATIONAL ARCHIVES]

**Q.** What change in ambulance design instituted by the surgeon general, Charles S. Tripler, after First Bull Run improved ambulance service somewhat?

**A.** He replaced the unsafe two-wheel vehicles with four-wheel models.

———◆———

**Q.** How many amendments to the Constitution were the direct result of the Civil War?

**A.** Three (Amendments Thirteen, Fourteen, and Fifteen).

———◆———

**Q.** What structure, completed in 1897, stands 150 feet tall and is the largest mausoleum in the nation?

**A.** Grant's tomb, in New York City.

# 8

# Places:
# Small and Large,
# Obscure and Famous

Q. The English-born entertainer Harry McCarthy wrote the popular southern song "The Bonnie Blue Flag" in the spring of 1861 and performed it for the first time in what city?

A. Jackson, Mississippi.

───────◆───────

Q. In what vast uninhabited marshy area of tangled forest and underbrush west of Chancellorsville, Virginia, did Grant propose to fight it out "if it takes all summer"?

A. The Wilderness.

───────◆───────

Q. Jefferson Davis regarded what site in his home state as "the Gibraltar of the West"?

A. Vicksburg, Mississippi.

───────◆───────

Q. What city held the only gas works of the Confederacy capable of inflating observation balloons?

A. Richmond, Virginia.

───────◆───────

Q. What small community was completely transformed by General Grant, who made it his headquarters and the "nerve center" of the Union for the final ten months of the war?

A. City Point, Virginia.

**Q.** What was the name of the 800-acre plantation on the Mississippi River owned by Jefferson Davis?

**A.** Briarwood.

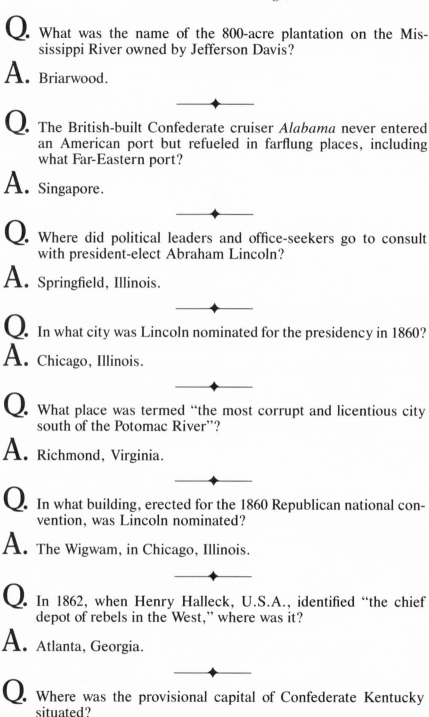

**Q.** The British-built Confederate cruiser *Alabama* never entered an American port but refueled in farflung places, including what Far-Eastern port?

**A.** Singapore.

**Q.** Where did political leaders and office-seekers go to consult with president-elect Abraham Lincoln?

**A.** Springfield, Illinois.

**Q.** In what city was Lincoln nominated for the presidency in 1860?

**A.** Chicago, Illinois.

**Q.** What place was termed "the most corrupt and licentious city south of the Potomac River"?

**A.** Richmond, Virginia.

**Q.** In what building, erected for the 1860 Republican national convention, was Lincoln nominated?

**A.** The Wigwam, in Chicago, Illinois.

**Q.** In 1862, when Henry Halleck, U.S.A., identified "the chief depot of rebels in the West," where was it?

**A.** Atlanta, Georgia.

**Q.** Where was the provisional capital of Confederate Kentucky situated?

**A.** Russellville.

**Q.** On April 2, 1863, several hundred women and children caused a "Bread Riot" in what southern city?

**A.** Richmond, Virginia.

——◆——

**Q.** What two rivers contributed to the strategic importance of Harpers Ferry, Virginia, now West Virginia?

**A.** The Potomac and the Shenandoah.

——◆——

**Q.** What fertile region, the "Breadbasket of the Confederacy," was systematically destroyed by General Sheridan's army?

**A.** The Shenandoah Valley of Virginia.

——◆——

**Q.** What home, one of the few dwellings of Manassas, Virginia, was directly in front of McDowell's forces?

**A.** The Henry House.

——◆——

**Q.** What state was invaded by Braxton Bragg in expectation that multitudes would flock to join the Confederate forces?

**A.** Kentucky, in the fall of 1862.

——◆——

**Q.** In April 1861, what city was first on the list of targets considered important by Lincoln?

**A.** Charleston, South Carolina.

——◆——

**Q.** The sunken road that became known as Bloody Lane was near what Maryland town?

**A.** Sharpsburg, where the battle of Antietam was fought.

——◆——

**Q.** Where did the first significant military action by Union forces take place, on May 24, 1861?

**A.** Alexandria, Virginia.

*Abraham Lincoln took the oath of office in the unfinished U.S. Capitol. Windows facing the spot at which he stood were filled with sharpshooters, but the heavily pro-southern residents of the city made no attempt at violence. Deeply superstitious, the president regarded the unfinished building as an omen; until work on it was completed, he believed he would continue to guide the nation.*

**Q.** Into what state did Henry Halleck, U.S.A., lead troops without authorization?

**A.** Maryland, to defend Washington, in September 1862.

**Q.** In 1862 the New England Freedman's Aid Society began a school to educate newly liberated blacks in what state?

**A.** South Carolina.

**Q.** Marye's Height, an important strategic site, was near what town?

**A.** Fredericksburg, Virginia.

**Q.** Named military governor of what state, Andrew J. Hamilton began cotton export there?

**A.** Texas.

**Q.** At what Virginia fort were runaway slaves first designated "contraband of war" when the Union commander discovered they had been used in building Confederate fortifications?

**A.** Fort Monroe.

**Q.** What was the southernmost Atlantic Coast point in Confederate territory to be captured by Federal forces?

**A.** St. Augustine, Florida.

**Q.** Near the Hornet's Nest and the Bloody Pond was the Peach Orchard whose blossoms, cut by bullets, fell like pink snow onto what battle site?

**A.** Shiloh.

**Q.** The Baltimore Riots, April 19, 1861, angered the South and inspired the poet James Ryder Randall to write what song?

**A.** "Maryland, My Maryland."

---

**Q.** What was the northernmost point in Union territory to be raided by Confederates?

**A.** St. Albans, Vermont.

---

**Q.** What city was the scene of purported plots to kill Lincoln as he journeyed to his inauguration?

**A.** Baltimore, Maryland.

---

**Q.** In what city was the provisional government of the Confederate States of America formed?

**A.** Montgomery, Alabama.

---

**Q.** Late in 1862, what city was regarded in Washington as the "best starting point for Chattanooga"?

**A.** Nashville, Tennessee.

---

**Q.** Late in 1862 to what state did Jefferson Davis proclaim an offer to "help throw off the foreign yoke"?

**A.** Maryland.

---

**Q.** Into what state did a disproportionately large number of carpetbaggers descend after the war?

**A.** Mississippi.

---

**Q.** What northern states were invaded by Robert E. Lee as the head of the Army of Northern Virginia?

**A.** Maryland and Pennsylvania.

Part of Atlanta's military significance came from its role as a transportation center. Goods produced by the farms and small factories of the South poured into the fast-growing town. By means of the single-track Western and Atlantic Railroad, supplies went from Atlanta to Confederate armies. Naturally, therefore, once Gen. William T. Sherman was in control, he saw to it that his sappers put Atlanta's railroads out of commission.

Q. What Confederate capital was over half destroyed by retreating Southerners who set fire to cotton bales to impede the enemy?

A. Columbia, South Carolina.

———◆———

Q. As the principal speaker, the well-known orator Edward Everett delivered a long address on November 19, 1863, at the dedication of what battlefield?

A. Gettysburg, Pennsylvania.

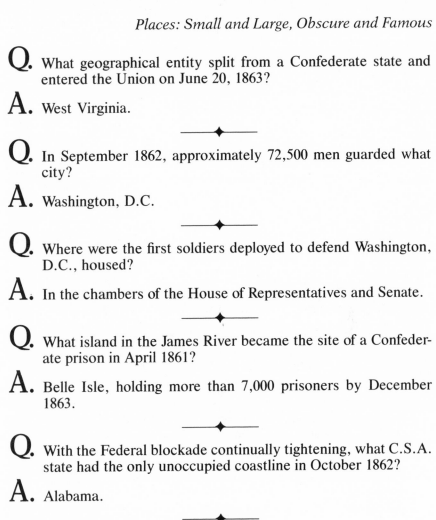

**Q.** What geographical entity split from a Confederate state and entered the Union on June 20, 1863?

**A.** West Virginia.

◆

**Q.** In September 1862, approximately 72,500 men guarded what city?

**A.** Washington, D.C.

◆

**Q.** Where were the first soldiers deployed to defend Washington, D.C., housed?

**A.** In the chambers of the House of Representatives and Senate.

◆

**Q.** What island in the James River became the site of a Confederate prison in April 1861?

**A.** Belle Isle, holding more than 7,000 prisoners by December 1863.

◆

**Q.** With the Federal blockade continually tightening, what C.S.A. state had the only unoccupied coastline in October 1862?

**A.** Alabama.

◆

**Q.** Where was the artificial island topped by an unfinished fort which was wanted by both South and North?

**A.** In the harbor of Charleston, South Carolina, holding Fort Sumter.

◆

**Q.** What river was jokingly called the "Chicken Hominy"?

**A.** The Chickahominy, in Virginia.

◆

**Q.** What Union military department stretched from the Ohio-Illinois border to the Rocky Mountains?

**A.** The Western Department, created July 3, 1861.

**Q.** In what city was the commanding general of the Western Department stationed in 1861?

**A.** St. Louis, Missouri.

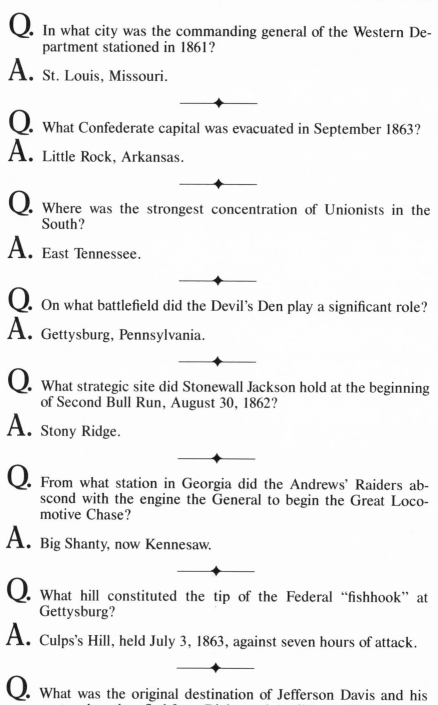

**Q.** What Confederate capital was evacuated in September 1863?

**A.** Little Rock, Arkansas.

**Q.** Where was the strongest concentration of Unionists in the South?

**A.** East Tennessee.

**Q.** On what battlefield did the Devil's Den play a significant role?

**A.** Gettysburg, Pennsylvania.

**Q.** What strategic site did Stonewall Jackson hold at the beginning of Second Bull Run, August 30, 1862?

**A.** Stony Ridge.

**Q.** From what station in Georgia did the Andrews' Raiders abscond with the engine the General to begin the Great Locomotive Chase?

**A.** Big Shanty, now Kennesaw.

**Q.** What hill constituted the tip of the Federal "fishhook" at Gettysburg?

**A.** Culps's Hill, held July 3, 1863, against seven hours of attack.

**Q.** What was the original destination of Jefferson Davis and his party when they fled from Richmond April 2, 1865?

**A.** Danville, Virginia.

**Q.** Where did Stonewall Jackson win a double victory in battles on two consecutive days, June 8–9, 1862?

**A.** Cross Keys and Port Republic, Virginia.

———◆———

**Q.** As Trans-Mississippi head, Theophilus Holmes, U.S.A., expected to hold what states with fifty thousand men?

**A.** Texas, Missouri, New Mexico, Arkansas, Indian Territory, and West Louisiana.

———◆———

**Q.** In what Federal prison was Jefferson Davis held for two years after the war?

**A.** Fort Monroe, Virginia.

———◆———

**Q.** What river, flooded by spring rains, slowed Sherman's advance upon Atlanta?

**A.** The Chattahoochee.

———◆———

**Q.** Missionary Ridge is on the eastern slope of what mountain?

**A.** Lookout Mountain, at Chattanooga, Tennessee.

———◆———

**Q.** What infamous Confederate prison incarcerated political prisoners, including "semi-Yankees"?

**A.** Castle Thunder in Richmond.

———◆———

**Q.** What site, made nationally prominent by abolitionist John Brown, was shifted from one state to another?

**A.** Harpers Ferry, Virginia, later in West Virginia.

———◆———

**Q.** What state did C.S.A. cavalryman J. E. B. Stuart raid in October 1862?

**A.** Pennsylvania, in his Chambersburg raid.

**Q.** Three stone bridges across what waterway gained lasting fame in September 1862?

**A.** Antietam Creek, near Sharpsburg, Maryland.

◆

**Q.** Early in the war, toward what Virginia town did Washington civilians head with picnic lunches to watch a battle?

**A.** Manassas (First Bull Run).

◆

**Q.** What was the starting point of Union forces that marched to defeat at First Bull Run?

**A.** Arlington Mansion (seized from Mrs. R. E. Lee).

◆

**Q.** Where did Lincoln go in July 1862 to consult with Maj. Gen. George B. McClellan?

**A.** Harrison's Landing, Virginia.

◆

**Q.** What river city was under siege by U. S. Grant for six weeks?

**A.** Vicksburg, Mississippi.

◆

**Q.** Where did opposing armies fight fiercely in November 1863 for an entire day, with vision limited by fog and mist?

**A.** Lookout Mountain, at Chattanooga, Tennessee.

◆

**Q.** Where did Abraham Lincoln and U. S. Grant first meet face to face?

**A.** The White House, at 9:30 P.M., March 8, 1864.

◆

**Q.** What state provided the Union with only about five hundred fighting men, who served in the Second Massachusetts Cavalry?

**A.** California.

[HARPER'S WEEKLY]

*Charleston was one of the Confederate targets Abraham Lincoln personally pinpointed early in the war. The city was much more than a hotbed of secession; the port was one of the nation's finest and busiest. Repeated Union attempts to take over the city failed, and it did not fall until February 1865. Here the USS* Weehawken *(left foreground) leads a futile assault upon Confederate positions.*

Q. During the Civil War, what was the westernmost region represented by a delegate to the C.S.A. Congress?

A. The Territory of Arizona.

———◆———

Q. Late in 1862, voters of what state adopted a constitutional provision that barred immigration of blacks?

A. Illinois, the land of Lincoln.

———◆———

Q. The name of what promontory at Gettysburg was unfortunately symbolic for Confederate forces?

A. Cemetery Ridge.

## Engagements and Battles

Engagements between Union and Confederate troops were spread across the nation. Below are the states and the number of engagements that took place in them:

Alabama, 78
Arizona, 4
Arkansas, 167
California, 6
Colorado, 4
Dakota Territory, 11
District of Columbia, 1
Florida, 32
Georgia, 108
Idaho, 1
Illinois, 1
Indiana, 4
Indian Territory, 17
Kansas, 7
Kentucky, 138
Louisiana, 118
Maryland, 30

Minnesota, 6
Mississippi, 186
Missouri, 244
Nebraska, 2
Nevada, 2
North Carolina, 85
New Mexico, 19
New York, 1
Oregon, 4
Pennsylvania, 9
South Carolina, 60
Tennessee, 298
Texas, 14
Utah, 1
Virginia, 519
Washington, 1
West Virginia, 80

Q. Across the borders of what states does Lookout Mountain sprawl?

A. Alabama, Georgia, and Tennessee.

———◆———

Q. What South Carolina fort, turned into a Confederate prison, held Federal officers captured in early engagements?

A. Castle Pinckney, at Charleston, South Carolina.

———◆———

Q. With regular army troops fighting elsewhere, short-term volunteers in the Colorado Territory committed a great massacre of Arapaho and Cheyenne Indians at what place?

A. Sand Creek.

**Q.** Where was a U.S. naval facility surrendered to Confederates on April 12, 1861, by James F. Armstrong?

**A.** Pensacola, Florida.

———◆———

**Q.** At what headquarters did Lincoln personally review troops in June 1864?

**A.** City Point, Virginia, headquarters of U. S. Grant.

———◆———

**Q.** What was the immediate objective of Union forces sent to engage in the first pitched battle?

**A.** Fairfax Court House, Virginia.

———◆———

**Q.** Union capture of what city is credited with making the greatest contribution to Abraham Lincoln's reelection in 1864?

**A.** Atlanta, Georgia.

———◆———

**Q.** At what site was Thomas J. Jackson first called Stonewall?

**A.** Henry Hill, Manassas, Virginia.

———◆———

**Q.** What was the only part of Texas under Union control when Lincoln appointed a military governor of the state?

**A.** Galveston Harbor.

———◆———

**Q.** Where was Fort Fillmore, occupied in early 1861 by a Federal garrison twice the size of that in Washington?

**A.** Forty miles north of El Paso, Texas.

———◆———

**Q.** What C.S.A. position was attacked by Union forces in March 1865, with Lincoln watching the action?

**A.** Fort Stedman, Virginia.

Q. What vast area of the United States was surrendered by Gen. David Twiggs to a posse of C.S.A. civilians?

A. Texas.

———◆———

Q. In September 1862, where did battlefield casualties cause the famous Stonewall Division, C.S.A., to have three commanders within minutes?

A. Antietam.

———◆———

Q. Where was the largest Confederate prison in Texas, which at one time held 5,000 men?

A. Camp Ford, northwest of Tyler.

———◆———

Q. Upon the capture of Jefferson Davis by Federal troops, where were his children sent?

A. To Canada, for refuge with Varina Davis's mother.

———◆———

Q. Although Lincoln promised never to invade it, what state was repeatedly ravaged by Federal and Confederate armies?

A. Kentucky.

———◆———

Q. After the war, while most Southerners accepted their fate, a colony of former Confederate slave owners was established in what South American state?

A. São Paolo, Brazil.

———◆———

Q. At war's end, Gen. Joseph Shelby and some members of his Iron Brigade offered their services to what government but were refused for political reasons?

A. Mexico, under Emperor Maximilian.

**Q.** What Gettysburg hill, initially held by Federal forces with six guns, fell to Confederates near dusk on July 2, 1863?

**A.** The Devil's Den, named for grotesque-appearing boulders.

———◆———

**Q.** For having delivered what "key site" did Jefferson Davis congratulate Edmund K. Smith in September 1862?

**A.** Cumberland Gap, between Tennessee and Kentucky.

———◆———

**Q.** Where is Pigeon Mountain, occupied by Confederate general Braxton Bragg, September 9–10, 1863?

**A.** West of Missionary Ridge, one of four mountains shielding Chattanooga, Tennessee, from the south.

———◆———

**Q.** Big Round Top, a knob 785 feet high, was of vital strategic importance in what battle?

**A.** Gettysburg.

———◆———

**Q.** What Confederate capital was twice burned by the Federals, in May and July 1863?

**A.** Jackson, Mississippi.

———◆———

**Q.** What U.S. territories stretched to the Pacific Ocean during much of the war?

**A.** The Territory of Utah and the Territory of New Mexico.

———◆———

**Q.** What major battle site is situated less than thirty air miles from Washington, D.C.?

**A.** Bull Run, or Manassas, Virginia.

———◆———

**Q.** At what site did Confederate bullets kill a soldier standing close to President Lincoln?

**A.** Fort Stevens, Washington, D.C.

Q. Where was the Federal First Corps "shot to pieces" in the September 17, 1862, battle of Antietam?

A. The Cornfield.

———◆———

Q. Initially all but defenseless, what Union city eventually was protected by sixty enclosed forts?

A. Washington, D.C.

———◆———

Q. On what bluff did crew members of the CSS *Virginia* (USS *Merrimac)* man a battery of field artillery?

A. Drewry's Bluff (or Fort Darling), Virginia, June 15, 1862.

———◆———

Q. What Confederate cavalryman reached the outskirts of Washington, D.C., on July 11, 1864?

A. Jubal Early.

———◆———

Q. Sherman's March to the Sea ended at what southern city?

A. Savannah, Georgia.

———◆———

Q. Where is Robert E. Lee believed to have said, "It is well that war is so terrible; we should grow too fond of it"?

A. At Fredericksburg, December 1862.

———◆———

Q. To what site did Mary Todd Lincoln go with her husband in July 1864 "in order to watch the action"?

A. Fort Stevens, near Washington, D.C.

———◆———

Q. Just five days after Georgia seceded, eight hundred members of the state militia seized what big arsenal?

A. Augusta Arsenal.

[HARPER'S WEEKLY]

*Situated only about one hundred miles from Richmond, capital of the C.S.A., Washington was considered by Union leaders to be vulnerable to attack. At the time Lincoln called 75,000 militia into Federal service, the city was undefended. Early contingents of Union soldiers slept in the Capitol, the Treasury Building, and even the White House. Within months, the civilian population was greatly outnumbered by soldiers, many of whom were personally reviewed by the president* (here standing lower left). *Before the war was over, Washington was one of the most heavily fortified cities in the world.*

Q. What three cities did Lincoln call "the brain, heart, and bowels of the rebellion"?

A. Richmond, Virginia; Chattanooga, Tennessee; Vicksburg, Mississippi.

———◆———

Q. What unfinished building dominated the skyline of Washington at Lincoln's first inauguration?

A. The Capitol, where he took the oath of office.

**Q.** In what battle was Snodgrass Hill regarded as being of strategic significance?

**A.** Chickamauga, Georgia, September 19–23, 1863.

———◆———

**Q.** What was the chief objective of the October 1862 raid into Pennsylvania by J. E. B. Stuart, C.S.A.?

**A.** To cut the Cumberland Valley Railroad, which was supplying McClellan's army.

———◆———

**Q.** On what battlefield was the Bloody Angle?

**A.** Spotsylvania, Virginia, May 12, 1864.

———◆———

**Q.** Following surrender, where was Jefferson Davis captured by Federal troops?

**A.** Near Ocilla, Georgia, about seventy miles north of the Florida state line.

———◆———

**Q.** In what northern city did Confederates under Jubal Early burn an estimated four hundred buildings on July 30–31, 1864?

**A.** Chambersburg, Pennsylvania.

———◆———

**Q.** At what point on the James River did Benjamin Butler, U.S.A., try to cut a 174-yard canal in August 1864?

**A.** At Dutch Gap, Virginia.

———◆———

**Q.** After his home had been shelled during First Bull Run, where did Wilmer McLean move his family so "the sound of battle would never reach them"?

**A.** Appomattox Court House, where the Confederacy's surrender took place in his parlor.

# 9

# Weapons:
# Old and New,
# Deadly and Harmless

**Q.** What was the caliber of the bayonet-equipped Enfield rifle-musket, usually listed simply as "rifle"?

**A.** .557-caliber, for use with smooth-sided minié balls.

———◆———

**Q.** What distinguished the eight-inch seacoast howitzer, model 1841, from counterparts used in the field?

**A.** A swell at the muzzle.

———◆———

**Q.** What was the maximum range of a shell from the gigantic twenty-inch Rodman smoothbore gun?

**A.** About 3.5 miles.

———◆———

**Q.** Thirteen-inch seacoast mortars could send a 220-pound bomb 4,325 yards if elevated to what degree?

**A.** 45 degrees.

———◆———

**Q.** How many guns were expected to be fired as a salute to the U.S. flag when Fort Sumter was surrendered?

**A.** One hundred, but firing stopped after the fiftieth gun exploded.

Q. What was the name of some naval vessels, both Federal and Confederate, that were provided with iron prows?

A. Ram.

———◆———

Q. What blade did naval personnel use in hand-to-hand combat?

A. The cutlass.

---

### All Four Evangelists Roared

The Rev. William N. Pendleton became pastor of Grace Episcopal Church in Richmond, Virginia, in 1853 and retained the post until his death thirty years later. When war broke out, he asked for and was granted a leave of absence. Without military experience, he was elected captain of the Rockbridge Artillery, where he named the four cannons of his battery Matthew, Mark, Luke, and John.

Each of the four evangelists roared so effectively that the pastor on leave, soon made a colonel, was chosen by Joseph E. Johnston to serve as his chief of artillery.

---

Q. During the C.S.A. retreat to Appomattox, who was killed by James Dearing in a rare pistol duel?

A. Lt. Col. Theodore Read, U.S.A.

———◆———

Q. Where were virtually all Civil War cannon loaded?

A. At the muzzle, with breech-loaders becoming standard by 1875.

———◆———

Q. What new bullet was largely responsible for the huge casualties in Civil War battles because of its greater accuracy and the army's lag in devising new tactics to compensate for it?

A. The minié bullet, called the minié ball.

**Q.** When a Federal commander planned an attack, how much ammunition was standard issue for infantry?

**A.** Sixty rounds per man.

---

**Q.** What offensive device did Benjamin F. Butler, U.S.A., find useless against Fort Fisher, North Carolina?

**A.** A barge loaded with 235 tons of powder, which exploded harmlessly when it went aground 800 yards early.

---

**Q.** At Haines Bluff on the Mississippi River, what novel "torpedoes" were used by Confederate defenders?

**A.** Fused whiskey demijohns filled with powder.

---

**Q.** Hidden explosives, such as mines, torpedoes, and incendiaries, were called by what term?

**A.** Infernal machines.

---

**Q.** How were models of cannon identified to be distinguished from one another?

**A.** By the number of inches in their bore diameters, or by the weight of projectiles thrown by them.

---

**Q.** Lacking sufficient artillery, southern defenders often had to use what simulated weapons?

**A.** Quaker guns, logs painted and positioned to look like cannon.

---

**Q.** What Confederate colonel spent $28,000 of his own money to equip the Twenty-second Alabama with fine Enfield rifles?

**A.** Zachariah C. Deas.

Q. Confederate general Gabriel Rains was rebuked by his superiors for using what devices at Yorktown, Virginia, in 1862?

A. Buried land mines, considered ungentlemanly conduct of war.

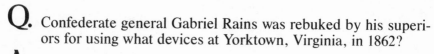

Q. Adopted in 1861, what was the most widely used shoulder arm of the U.S. Army?

A. The Springfield rifle.

Q. Who built for the C.S.A. a steam-powered cannon that interested Lincoln, but no fighting men?

A. Ross Winans, of Baltimore, Maryland.

Q. On what part of a big gun were culprits often spread-eagled for hours as punishment?

A. Carriage wheel.

Q. The traditional infantry charge with what weapon became obsolete during the Civil War?

A. Bayonet.

Q. What Massachusetts armory was producing 300,000 rifles annually by 1864?

A. Springfield Armory.

Q. What strategic movement was developed in an attempt by attackers to avoid deadly long-range rifle fire?

A. The envelopment, against the flank of a fixed position.

Q. Why was the Colt repeating rifle unpopular with both Federal and Confederate troops?

A. Firing of one round often set off all the rest, proving dangerous to the user.

Pvt. John Gilleland of the Mitchell Thunderbolts had a great idea. As a member of an elite home guard unit, the businessman was sure his inspiration would bring a quick end to the war. He took his concept to an Athens, Georgia, foundry and persuaded artisans to turn out a double-barreled cannon. Fired simultaneously, its barrels would eject a pair of balls connected with a chain in order to "mow down Yankees as a scythe cuts wheat." Legend has it that in its sole test firing, balls whizzed around in erratic fashion and killed three Thunderbolts. Now it may be the only piece of Civil War ordnance to be honored with its personal historical marker. For years, it has been fired with blank charges during local civic celebrations. Mayor Ralph M. Snow (shown here) was inspecting balls to be sure they were not linked by a chain before the weapon was used once more.

**Q.** Columbiad heavy artillery pieces were banded by Confederates so they could send a 225-pound ball what distance?

**A.** A maximum of 1,800 yards.

——◆——

**Q.** Particularly effective in the siege of Petersburg, the heavy thirteen-inch mortar nicknamed the Dictator was mounted on what contraption?

**A.** A railroad flatcar.

——◆——

**Q.** After Fredericksburg, when Confederates gleaned the battlefield for small arms, how many did they pick up?

**A.** Approximately 11,000.

——◆——

**Q.** What fierce-looking "repeater cannon" failed to live up to its inventor's claims?

**A.** The Rafael cannon.

——◆——

**Q.** What kind of shells were tested in June 1863 when President Lincoln visited the headquarters of Joseph Hooker?

**A.** Incendiaries.

——◆——

**Q.** What was the maximum weight of a shell for a ten-inch Columbiad?

**A.** 128 pounds.

——◆——

**Q.** About how much did a ten-inch Columbiad of standard construction weigh?

**A.** Fifteen thousand pounds.

——◆——

**Q.** How were the iron tires of caissons and field artillery muffled for silence in retreat or advance?

**A.** They were wrapped in blankets.

**Q.** Poorly supplied Confederate horse soldiers preferred to use what privately owned shoulder arm?

**A.** Sawed-off shotgun.

---

**Q.** What was the regulation weight of powder used to fire a shell from a ten-inch Columbiad?

**A.** Eighteen pounds.

---

**Q.** Although defenders of Fort Sumter had three eighteen-inch Columbiads on hand, how many did they succeed in firing?

**A.** One.

---

**Q.** Beyond what size were cannon not practical for use in the field?

**A.** Twenty-four pounds.

---

**Q.** What simple piece of iron, driven into the vent of a muzzle-loading cannon, effectively disabled it?

**A.** A spike.

---

**Q.** What was the effective range of case shot, designed to explode soon after being fired?

**A.** About 500 to 1,500 yards as antipersonnel shot.

---

**Q.** When up to full strength, a field battery commanded by a captain mustered 155 men and how many guns of the same caliber?

**A.** Six.

---

**Q.** What metal was typically used in casting a smoothbore for field use?

**A.** Bronze.

**Q.** What was the popular name for the fused shell lobbed by a mortar?

**A.** Bomb.

---

**Q.** What federal installation in Georgia, seized in January 1861 only five days after the state seceded, became a major supplier of Confederate materiel and ammunition?

**A.** Augusta Arsenal.

---

**Q.** What innovative practice did artillerists devise to make their cannons effective antiballoon guns?

**A.** Tails of cannon were placed in ditches to boost the height of their firing range.

---

**Q.** What special service unit was attached to a battery of field artillery to service guns, caissons, and limbers?

**A.** A traveling forge.

---

**Q.** How were big guns on some warships of the Mississippi River casemated?

**A.** Between their big side-wheel boxes.

---

**Q.** What was the term for the opening in a fortification whose sides flared outward for the benefit of a heavy gun inside?

**A.** Embrasure.

---

**Q.** What was the chief target of the (infrequently fired) heavy guns used by defenders of Fort Sumter?

**A.** Morris Island.

---

**Q.** How much did a standard shell for an English-made Whitworth cannon weigh?

**A.** Twelve pounds.

---◆---

**Q.** What rifle muskets did both sides import from England, made by private contractors as the British government did not wish to be involved?

**A.** Enfields, 400,000 units on each side.

---◆---

**Q.** Southern snipers using the Whitworth rifle were greatly feared because it was demonstrated at Petersburg that a projectile fired over a mile away deviated from its target only how far?

**A.** About twelve feet.

---◆---

**Q.** Early on the second day that Fort Sumter was bombarded, what projectiles did attackers begin using?

**A.** Red-hot shot, designed to set the fort on fire.

---◆---

**Q.** Where did Confederates first use Quaker guns?

**A.** Centreville, Virginia, in July 1861.

---◆---

**Q.** What device was most effective in discovering that an imposing-looking battery held only Quaker guns?

**A.** An observation balloon.

---◆---

**Q.** What deadly device improvised by Federals in Charleston on August 28, 1864, proved to be harmless?

**A.** A raft loaded with gunpowder plus a burning fuse.

---◆---

**Q.** When ammunition grew scarce in the C.S.A., where did munitions makers get a new supply of lead?

**A.** From window weights of mansions.

[*LOSSING'S PICTORIAL HISTORY OF THE CIVIL WAR*]

WINANS'S STEAM-GUN.

*Wealthy Ross Winans of Baltimore, a strong backer of the Confederate cause, decided to invest part of his fortune in what became perhaps the most unusual heavy weapon of the era. His patented steam cannon attracted the interested attention of Abraham Lincoln. Reputedly, Lincoln offered amnesty to Winans in exchange for the plans from which his steam cannon was built. When it was assembled, trained horses bolted at the sight of it, and strong men shuddered. But there's no record that it produced a single battlefield casualty.*

Q. When David D. Porter, U.S.N., built a dummy warship in a bid to dupe Confederates, how was it armed?

A. With large logs made to look like cannons.

———◆———

Q. What did Confederates call their time bomb used to destroy Union docks at City Point, Virginia, on August 9, 1864?

A. A horological torpedo.

———◆———

Q. At Fort Fisher, North Carolina, what big gun was used by defenders in a move to keep attacking Federal warships at bay?

A. An eight-inch Armstrong, rifled.

———◆———

Q. What projectiles, designed to whirl toward their targets, looked lethal but were seldom, if ever, effectively used?

A. Bar shot and chain shot, two balls linked by a bar or by a chain.

———◆———

Q. What device was used against wooden ships to pierce the hull and smolder inside, eventually causing a fire?

A. Hot shot, heated iron.

———◆———

Q. When Federal forces occupied Charleston, South Carolina, on February 18, 1865, how many big guns were captured?

A. Two hundred fifty.

———◆———

Q. Of what material were cartridges for the famous Colt revolver made?

A. Paper or linen (or loose ball and powder and percussion cap).

———◆———

Q. At Fredericksburg, Virginia, in December 1862, with what did Maj. John Pelham, C.S.A., reply to twenty-four pieces of field artillery?

A. One twelve-pound brass Napoleon.

———◆———

Q. With metal scarce by mid-1862, what new source of raw material for cannon was found in Mississippi?

A. Brass and iron plantation bells.

———◆———

Q. To unhorse Federal cavalry, what unconventional weapons were used by rifle-short Confederates at Falling Waters, Maryland, on July 14, 1863?

A. Axes and fence rails.

**Q.** What field artillery projectile with attached powder bag or cartridge could be loaded as one piece?

**A.** Fixed ammunition.

---

**Q.** In the naval battle to recapture Galveston, the Confederates were victorious using what unorthodox tactics?

**A.** Hand-to-hand combat between Federal sailors and Texas cavalry acting as riflemen.

---

**Q.** What head of the Bureau of Ordnance and Hydrography for the Confederate navy invented a highly regarded heavy artillery gun that bore his name?

**A.** John Mercer Brooke, inventor of the Brooke rifle.

---

**Q.** What inaccurate weapon, largely used by Confederates, was all but useless except at very close range?

**A.** The .69-caliber smoothbore musket.

---

**Q.** How many Confederate casualties were inflicted when the magazine of the abandoned USS *Westfield* was fired?

**A.** None; it blew up the ship prematurely.

---

**Q.** When David Farragut, U.S.N., set out to take New Orleans, how many guns were mounted on his ships?

**A.** 243, mostly heavy.

---

**Q.** What was the major Northern center for manufacture of heavy mortars?

**A.** Pittsburgh, Pennsylvania.

---

**Q.** What Union general, whose name has also entered the language in another context, invented and manufactured a popular

Robert P. Parrott, a West Point graduate in the class of 1824, decided that a reinforcing band on the breech of a cannon would double its strength. Working as a foundry superintendent, he managed to produce a ten-pounder in 1860. It was so successful that he was soon turning out heavier pieces. At First Bull Run the thirty-pound Parrott gun (shown above, at right) was first used in battle. Had field pieces of this sort not been present at the battle, the Confederate victory might have been so overwhelming that Union lawmakers would have demanded that their president sit down at the conference table and talk peace. Instead, Lincoln called for a vast increase in size of the regular army and navy, plus an additional 300,000 volunteers. Since First Bull Run did not end the conflict, Parrott continued working; by war's end, his guns were being used in every theater. A few of his biggest threw 300 pounds of iron from fortresses, mostly coastal.

carbine that was the first to use a metallic cartridge rather than a paper one?

A. Ambrose Burnside, who originated the Burnside carbine and the sideburn hair style.

**Q.** In what city were most of the mortar beds used by Union troops manufactured?

**A.** New York City.

---

**Q.** What was the fate of the CSS *Louisiana*?

**A.** Poorly designed and still incomplete, it was sent against U.S. naval forces advancing on New Orleans and was blown up to avoid capture.

---

**Q.** What was the armament of the CSS *Mississippi*, one of the first true "dreadnoughts"?

**A.** Twenty big guns.

---

**Q.** What powerful gun could be broken down into components and transported on the backs of mules?

**A.** The 1841 mountain howitzer, a twelve-pounder.

---

**Q.** What was the most distinctive external feature of the Parrott gun?

**A.** A single reinforcing band on the breech.

---

**Q.** When Nathan B. Forrest, C.S.A., left Columbia, Tennessee, on a December 1862 raid, how were most of his men armed?

**A.** With flintlock muskets and shotguns.

---

**Q.** What was the smallest shell thrown by a gun named for inventor Robert P. Parrott?

**A.** Ten inches.

---

**Q.** Approximately how many small arms were captured when Georgia militia took the Federal arsenal at Augusta?

**A.** Twenty-two thousand rifles.

**Q.** What was the approximate weight of the largest projectile used in the biggest Parrott guns?

**A.** Three hundred pounds.

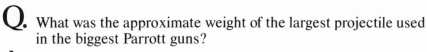

**Q.** How much powder was required to throw a 50.5-pound shell from a howitzer?

**A.** Four pounds.

**Q.** What was the fate of the CSS *Eastport*?

**A.** Stranded on the Red River, it was blown up by Confederates with 3,055 pounds of powder on April 26, 1864.

**Q.** A fifty-foot, cigar-shaped iron steamer, the CSS *David*, carried what armament?

**A.** A torpedo with one hundred pounds of explosives attached to the bow.

**Q.** If its muzzle was broken, what big gun, widely used by the Union, could be sawed smooth and still used?

**A.** The Parrott, easily operated by inexperienced crews.

**Q.** By what generic term did the Federals call all Confederate torpedo boats?

**A.** Davids, after the CSS *David*, a torpedo boat.

**Q.** Aboard the USS *Hartford*, David Farragut planned to drop what unique weapon on the CSS *Arkansas* to scuttle her?

**A.** The *Hartford's* heaviest anchor.

**Q.** What weapon did Stonewall Jackson first employ against Federals at Cedar Mountain, Virginia, on August 9, 1862?

**A.** His sword.

———◆———

**Q.** What was the hazard of firing rifles too rapidly?

**A.** Barrels became too hot to handle.

———◆———

**Q.** What was the limit of use of the Bormann time fuse, widely attached to artillery shells?

**A.** Five seconds.

———◆———

**Q.** When men of the Stonewall Brigade exhausted their supply of ammunition in September 1862, what weapons did they use against attacking Federal forces?

**A.** Rocks.

———◆———

**Q.** Victorious at Second Bull Run, Robert E. Lee captured how many weapons there?

**A.** 20,000 muskets and rifles and 20 cannon.

———◆———

**Q.** What was the weight of the projectile thrown by a thirteen-inch "seacoast" mortar?

**A.** 220 pounds, using a charge of 20 pounds of powder.

———◆———

**Q.** What was the standard device that was pulled to set off field artillery and siege guns?

**A.** A lanyard.

———◆———

**Q.** What was the most popular smoothbore field artillery piece on either side in the war?

**A.** The Napoleon howitzer, named for the French emperor Louis Napoleon, nephew of Napoleon I.

[HARPER'S WEEKLY]

*Abraham Lincoln refused to call it a war, insisting that it was only a rebellion. By whatever name, the conflict produced more new offensive devices than any other struggle up to that time. Confederates named a secretary of the navy when they had no warships; desperately trying to get the better of heavily armed Union vessels, they came up with the idea of an "infernal machine." In its earliest version* (shown here) *it consisted of a pair of chain-linked barrels from which canisters of gunpowder were suspended. Crude as they were, these primitive mines blew the bottoms out of a number of the enemy ships.*

Q. What were Pook turtles?

A. Seven Union ironclad gunboats designed by Samuel M. Pook for use on western rivers.

———◆———

Q. Why did violent thunderstorms sometimes stop the use of muskets and rifles in combat?

A. Cartridges became too wet to ignite.

—203—

Q. Where did Joseph E. Johnston, C.S.A., once briefly hold off attackers with a dummy gun?

A. At Munson's Hill, from which the dome of the Capitol in Washington was visible.

———◆———

Q. What breech-loading rifle was popular with some Federal commanders?

A. The Maynard carbine.

———◆———

Q. On August 30, 1862, where did Kirby Smith, C.S.A., capture nine guns and ten thousand small arms from William Nelson, U.S.A.?

A. Richmond, Kentucky.

### Sudden Death

Sentenced to death for his attack upon Harpers Ferry, Virginia, John Brown was imprisoned at some distance from the scaffold erected especially for him. On December 2, 1859, he rode jauntily to the place of his execution while perched on top of his own coffin.

———◆———

Lt. Lemuel Jeffries of the Ohio Volunteer Infantry recorded in his journal an account of two other coffins. Each was hastily constructed to hold the body of a condemned deserter.

On September 18, 1863, not far from Culpeper, Virginia, Pvt. Edward Latham and Pvt. George Elliot obeyed a gesture and sat down on their coffins. About eighteen feet away, members of a Zouave firing squad took careful aim and fired. Elliott toppled over at once, but marksmen missed Latham.

Two Zouaves stepped within four paces and again pulled their triggers. This time, their weapons did not fire. An angry officer who was in charge of the executions dashed forward and held his revolver against the head of

**Q.** Aside from manufacture and importation, where did metal-scarce Confederates manage to get weapons?

**A.** From defeated Federal forces.

———◆———

**Q.** In prototype submarines, designed by both the North and the South, how were their torpedoes to contact enemy ships?

**A.** Divers would screw the mines to the bottoms of the vessels.

———◆———

**Q.** When he invaded Maryland in September 1862, what was Robert E. Lee's greatest fear, which he communicated to President Davis?

**A.** "Getting out of ammunition."

the condemned man; wet priming caused the third failure to execute the deserter.

A fourth attempt succeeded, but by this time badly wounded Elliott was trying to sit up. Turning to him, the officer put his revolver so close to Elliott that when it was fired, flames from the gun set his clothing on fire. Only then were the bodies of the condemned men—both from the Connecticut Infantry Volunteers—placed in coffins, which were pushed into graves dug before the ceremonial executions began.

———◆———

Confederate private Seth Laughlin was more fortunate. Drafted despite his plea that he objected to war on religious grounds, he was soon court-martialed and ordered to face a firing squad. Near Petersburg, Virginia, on the day scheduled for his death, the devout Laughlin offered a fervent prayer for the souls of the men about to shoot him. Members of the firing squad were so moved that they refused to do their duty. Bewildered, the officer in charge decided, on the spot, to commute Laughlin's sentence to imprisonment; so the coffin prepared for his body remained empty.

**Q.** What Union-made weapon, now in the Museum of the Confederacy at Richmond, was presented to Col. George Martin, C.S.A.?

**A.** The repeating Henry rifle, picked up on a battlefield, was to be used "for the President's defense" as the war ended.

---

**Q.** What charge was made when Confederates sometimes put three large buckshot on top of a .69-caliber musket ball?

**A.** Buck and ball.

---

**Q.** When recruits failed to flock to Braxton Bragg during his 1862 invasion of Kentucky, what lament did he voice?

**A.** "We have fifteen thousand stands of arms—and no one to use them."

---

**Q.** What disaster with its second balloon ended the Confederacy's use of this form of aerial reconnaissance?

**A.** It floated away in a high wind.

---

**Q.** Why did some Union generals question the value of the new repeating carbines and rifles, such as the Spencer?

**A.** They were concerned about possibly wasting ammunition but accepted the statement that it was "easier to carry extra bullets than a stretcher."

---

**Q.** What weapon did Jeff Davis, U.S.A., borrow to kill William Nelson in the Galt House hotel, Louisville?

**A.** A pistol, seldom used in battle.

---

**Q.** For threatening to use what weapon was Philip H. Sheridan, U.S.A., suspended from West Point for a year?

**A.** A fixed bayonet, with which he chased a cadet officer.

**Q.** What started the fire that burned Atlanta, graphically depicted in the movie *Gone With the Wind*?

**A.** Retreating Confederate general John B. Hood's firing of an ninety-one-car ammunition train that ignited the nearby Atlanta Gas Works.

---

## Quaker Guns

In March 1862, C.S.A. general Joseph E. Johnston pulled his army in Virginia out of Centreville. Union scouts, who had watched from a distance, had advised against an attack because of Johnston's strong defenses. When the town was empty, troops under Gen. George B. McClellan immediately occupied it and found six earth forts bristling with Quaker guns, fake weapons made from logs. Similar formidable-appearing but harmless "cannon" fashioned from tree trunks and pasteboard cropped up at Munson's Hill and several other sites scattered from northern Virginia to Corinth, Mississippi.

---◆---

Kentucky-born partisan leader Adam R. Johnson, later a Confederate brigadier, led a band of just twelve men against heavily defended Newburg, Indiana, on July 18, 1862. Union forces gave up without a fight when they saw a huge cannon headed directly toward them. Because the weapon that led to the capture of Newburg had been fashioned from a wagon and pieces of stovepipe, Johnson gained the nickname "Stovepipe," which stuck to him for the rest of his life.

---◆---

Cmdr. David D. Porter reasoned that "what's good for the goose is good for the gander." Fighting on the Mississippi River, he rigged up a fake warship, then armed it with logs and bluffed commanders of enemy vessels into thinking they were outgunned. It is small wonder that leaders in Washington decided to make permanent his temporary rank of rear admiral.

**Q.** What repeating rifle, not widely used, evolved from the Colt revolver?

**A.** The Colt repeater, properly known as the Colt-Root.

---

**Q.** What wooden device was sometimes strapped to a round projectile for a tighter fit?

**A.** The sabot, or shoe, banded with leather or tin.

---

**Q.** How far could the roar of an artillery battle be heard under the best conditions?

**A.** More than ten miles.

---

**Q.** When out of communication with his commander, how could an officer learn where fighting had started?

**A.** By the sound of gunfire.

---

**Q.** What famous type of knife, seldom used in combat, was a badge of ferocity and useful for camp chores in both armies?

**A.** Bowie.

---

**Q.** When bayonets were used, which of the two types was preferred?

**A.** The angular bayonet over the heavy sword bayonet, which was discontinued in 1864.

---

**Q.** What special device was attached to some rifles of the Federal units known as Berdan's Sharpshooters?

**A.** A telescopic sight.

---

**Q.** Introduction in 1863 of the Spencer repeating carbine for cavalry spelled the end of the usefulness of what traditional weapon?

**A.** Single-shot muzzle loader.

---

**Q.** What charge was necessary for use of the twenty-inch Rodman smoothbore, throwing a shell of 1,080 pounds?

**A.** One hundred pounds of powder.

---

**Q.** Some observers believed that continuous firing of heavy guns precipitated what meteorological change?

**A.** Rainfall, even during a drought.

---

**Q.** What was the approximate range of a field howitzer with an eight-inch bore diameter, throwing a 50.5-pound shell?

**A.** Slightly more than 1,200 yards.

---

**Q.** What was the caliber of the Burnside carbines for which an estimated two million cartridges were made?

**A.** .54-caliber.

---

**Q.** What big guns defended Fort Fisher, North Carolina, the "Gibraltar of the Confederacy"?

**A.** Fifteen Columbiads, one 150-pounder Armstrong, and thirty-five smaller guns.

---

**Q.** What was the caliber of the Army Colt revolver, carried by Federal personnel of both army and navy?

**A.** .44-caliber.

---

**Q.** What distinguished the trajectory of the typical mortar from that of a weapon in a field artillery battery?

**A.** Mortar "bombs" could be accurately thrown in a high arc.

# 10

# War in the East

Q. What engagement is generally considered to have been Robert E. Lee's final offensive of the war?

A. Fort Stedman, Virginia, March 29, 1865.

◆

Q. What battle, at the time considered by some Federals to be a victory, became the excuse for issuing the preliminary Emancipation Proclamation in September 1862?

A. Antietam (Sharpsburg, Maryland).

◆

Q. At Spotsylvania Court House, Virginia, May 12, 1864, approximately how many casualties were counted within one square mile?

A. Twelve thousand.

◆

Q. By causing considerable mirth among watching Confederate soldiers across the Rappahanock River in January 1863, a bogged-down "advance" by Union troop was given what name?

A. Burnside's Mud March.

◆

Q. Where did Joseph E. Johnston, C.S.A., surrender his army to William Tecumseh Sherman, U.S.A.?

A. Durham Station, North Carolina, seven miles west of today's Durham, April 26, 1865.

*To see him decked out in a dress uniform adorned with medals, a person would think that Gen. Philip H. Sheridan was a Union equivalent of Robert E. Lee, going about the business of war in thoroughly genteel fashion. This was not the case. When he became commander of the Army of the Shenandoah, he took the assignment knowing that he would be expected to destroy anything that might aid the enemy. He and his men roared through the beautiful Shenandoah Valley in such fashion that when they ended their campaign, some of his weary troopers said, "We stripped the Valley to the bare earth; when we got through there weren't enough crumbs left to feed a pigeon." Sheridan labeled his "scorched earth" policy as humanitarian, on the grounds that starving Confederates would call a halt to the war.*

[NATIONAL ARCHIVES]

**Q.** What was the mile-wide C.S.A. salient at Spotsylvania where it took twenty-four Union divisions to destroy one C.S.A. division?

**A.** The Mule Shoe, which held out for twenty hours.

———◆———

**Q.** When Jubal Early, C.S.A., headed toward Washington in July 1864, where were his men delayed for a day?

**A.** At Monocacy, Maryland, by Brig. Gen. James Ricketts's men.

———◆———

**Q.** For the surrender at Appomattox, where General Grant wore his usual unbuttoned private's blouse, what did General Lee wear?

**A.** A new full-dress uniform with sash and jewel-studded sword.

**Q.** At Gettysburg, what hard lesson did cavalryman Jeb Stuart learn, which he heeded through the rest of his career?

**A.** Always stay in communication with his army.

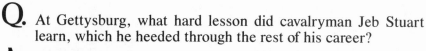

**Q.** In addition to 125 shops and barns, how many Chambersburg, Pennsylvania, homes were burned by C.S.A. raiders July 1864?

**A.** Approximately 275.

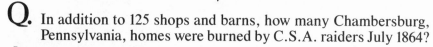

**Q.** What Union commander of the Department of Western Virginia was captured by partisans March 21, 1865?

**A.** Maj. Gen. George Crook (*b*. Ohio).

<hr>

**Q.** When Maj. Gen. Philip Kearny, U.S.A., rode into enemy lines and was killed, what happened to his body?

**A.** General Lee sent it to Federal forces under a flag of truce.

<hr>

**Q.** What uniforms did men under A. P. Hill, C.S.A., wear to deceive the enemy at Antietam?

**A.** New blue uniforms, captured at Harpers Ferry.

<hr>

**Q.** When the Federal Army of Virginia was created in June 1862, who was named to command it?

**A.** John Pope (*b*. Kentucky).

<hr>

**Q.** Stonewall Jackson was killed by "friendly fire" from what Southern unit?

**A.** The Eighth North Carolina.

<hr>

**Q.** About how many ascensions were made for the Union by members of observation balloon teams?

**A.** Slightly more than three thousand.

Q. The loss of what C.S.A. installation, with resulting recrimina-
tions, triggered two duels by Confederate officers?

A. Fort Huger, Virginia, April 18, 1863.

———◆———

Q. For how long was John Pope, U.S.A., commander of the Army
of Virginia?

A. Sixty-nine days.

---

### "Rebels Are Cream Puffs"

Abraham Lincoln's call for 75,000 volunteers in April
1861 brought a flurry of responses from northern editors.
Said the Philadelphia *Press*, "Rebels are a mere band of
ragamuffins. They will fly, like chaff, before our ap-
proach."

Readers of the New York *Times* were told that the
militia could be split three ways. With 25,000 men retained
in Washington and a similar body of troops sent to Cairo,
Illinois, the other one-third would "cross the Potomac to
Richmond, and burn out the rats there."

Subscribers to the Chicago *Tribune* read the editor's
brash boast, "Let the East get out of the way; this is a war
of the West. Illinois can whip the South by herself. We
insist on the battle being turned over to us."

---

Q. What Confederate installation was captured by Federals at
Chaffin's Farm, Virginia, September 29–30, 1864?

A. Fort Harrison, at a cost of 3,300 casualties.

———◆———

Q. When did the U.S. secretary of war, Edwin Stanton, order the
contents of the Washington arsenal sent to New York?

A. September 1862, after defeat of the Army of the Potomac.

**Q.** Beginning in 1862, President Lincoln directed his commanding generals to require what statements from citizens of occupied southern territory?

**A.** Loyalty oaths promising future allegiance (often totally disregarded).

---

**Q.** What did Confederates call the battle that Federals usually called the battle of White Oak Swamp, Virginia?

**A.** Nelson's Cross Roads, or New Market Road, June 30, 1862.

---

**Q.** What defeat was Pope summarizing for President Lincoln when he reported, "We have lost nothing; neither guns or wagons"?

**A.** Second Bull Run.

---

**Q.** When did Federal troops occupy Charleston, South Carolina, after it was evacuated by Confederates?

**A.** February 18, 1865.

---

**Q.** What West Point graduate, top man in the class of U. S. Grant, was relieved of duty for five months after Fredericksburg?

**A.** William Buel Franklin, relieved by Burnside (*b*. Pennsylvania).

---

**Q.** What did Confederates call the battle of Seven Pines, May 31–June 1, 1862?

**A.** Battle of Fair Oaks.

---

**Q.** When did General Grant succeed in cutting the last railroad linking Richmond with the lower South?

**A.** April 1, 1865.

---

**Q.** What independent body of volunteers operating under special orders made up the Loudoun Rangers?

**A.** Virginians from the Piedmont region who supported the Union.

———◆———

**Q.** What were the losses resulting from the project known as The Crater?

**A.** Union, 3,700; Confederate, 1,500.

———◆———

**Q.** From what town did McClellan notify Lincoln, "I have all the plans of the rebels"?

**A.** From Frederick, Maryland, after finding Lee's Lost Order.

———◆———

**Q.** What was the percentage of mortality, one of the highest in the war, suffered by the Seventh Michigan Infantry, which was attached to the Army of the Potomac?

**A.** 15.8 percent dead in battle, of wounds or disease, or in prison.

———◆———

**Q.** Who replaced Gen. Joseph Hooker on June 26, 1863?

**A.** Maj. Gen. George Gordon Meade (*b*. Spain).

———◆———

**Q.** Approximately how many men were engaged in battle at Fredericksburg or were available but held in reserve?

**A.** Two hundred thousand.

———◆———

**Q.** What small building at Salem Heights, Virginia, was converted into a Union hospital?

**A.** Salem Church, which was far too small for 4,700 casualties.

———◆———

**Q.** What was the term for a common corporal punishment of noncommissioned officers and enlisted men in both armies that required them to be trussed up with their knees bound under their chins and a stick inserted in their mouths?

**A.** Buck and gag.

**Q.** What Union commander, who reputedly was drinking rum while his men were slaughtered, was promoted in the aftermath of The Crater, Petersburg, Virginia, July 1864?

**A.** Brig. Gen. Edward Ferrero (*b.* Spain).

---

**Q.** By what modes of transportation did Lincoln go to Richmond on April 4, 1865, one day after the city was captured?

**A.** Aboard the USS *Malvern* and a gig rowed by twelve sailors.

---

**Q.** What commander was described in September 1862 as "dressed in seedy and dirty homespun, wearing 'a beggar's hat'"?

**A.** Stonewall Jackson.

---

**Q.** At Gaines Mill, Virginia, July 27, 1862, what Union charge was later seen as "a prelude to Pickett's Charge at Gettysburg"?

**A.** The suicidal charge of the Second and Fifth U.S. Cavalry.

---

**Q.** What engagement near a school, June 25, 1862, launched the Seven Days?

**A.** King's School House, or Oak Grove, Virginia.

---

**Q.** In what September 1862 engagement was the roar of cannon drowned out by the violence of a thunderstorm?

**A.** Chantilly, Virginia, September 1, 1862.

---

**Q.** Where were over one hundred men of the Fifth U.S. Colored Cavalry said to have been massacred on October 2, 1864?

**A.** At Saltville, Virginia.

**Q.** Discipline in both the Union and Confederate armies was often difficult to maintain because of what method of choosing troops?

**A.** Volunteer troops, all from a local area, elected their own leaders, who hesitated to be strict with their men.

---

**Q.** Where was the Union's famous Corcoran Legion, also called the Irish Legion, destroyed?

**A.** At Cold Harbor, Virginia, June 1864.

---

**Q.** What was the duration of the Overland campaign of the Army of the Potomac, a war of attrition directed by U. S. Grant?

**A.** Five weeks: May 4–June 12, 1864.

---

**Q.** Members of Stonewall Jackson's Second Corps, who in six weeks once marched 400 miles, fought five battles, and confused three Union generals, proudly called themselves by what name?

**A.** Old Jack's foot calvary.

---

**Q.** Where did Confederate seamen fight on land?

**A.** At Sayler's Creek, Virginia, where they briefly continued to fight after the surrender of Richard S. Ewell's army in April 1865.

---

**Q.** What other name is often applied to the battle of Brandy Station, Virginia, June 9, 1863?

**A.** The battle of Fleetwood Hill.

---

**Q.** Late in the war, in what conflict did men of two Union cavalry divisions fight on foot in dense woods?

**A.** Five Forks, Virginia, April 1, 1865.

*Perhaps because he seemed to be the penultimate southern gentleman from start to finish, Robert E. Lee is now almost as widely revered in the North as in the South. Usually fighting against overpowering odds, more than any other man he was responsible for the war dragging on for weary month after weary month. How did he do it? No one knows. His record prior to taking command of the Army of Northern Virginia would suggest that he would be mediocre, at best. During his period as commander of Virginia state forces, he spent most of his time and energy squabbling with subordinates instead of fighting, causing him to become widely known throughout the South as "Granny Lee," not "Yankee Killer."*

Q. Where was Robert E. Lee's first engagement of the war?

A. Cheat Mountain in western Virginia (now West Virginia), where Brig. Gen. Joseph J. Reynolds soundly defeated him.

———◆———

Q. Where did Union cavalry prove equal to their Confederate counterparts for the first time?

A. At Kelly's Ford, Virginia, March 17, 1863.

———◆———

Q. Where was the longest pontoon bridge in military history constructed?

A. Near Windmill Point on the James River, by Federal engineers, June 1864.

———◆———

Q. Approximately 1,700 Confederate soldiers were suffering from what disease just prior to doing battle at First Bull Run?

A. Measles.

———◆———

Q. Although wounded, what Union officer-hero helped pull a battery into position by hand, then died beside his guns at Gettysburg?

A. Maj. Alonzo Hersford Cushing (*b*. Wisconsin).

———◆———

Q. On what date were 8,000 Confederates captured, the most Americans ever taken prisoner in the United States after a battle?

A. "Black Thursday," April 6, 1865, at Sayler's Creek, Virginia.

———◆———

Q. At what army headquarters did Lincoln spend almost two weeks in March 1865?

A. City Point, Virginia, headquarters of U. S. Grant.

**Q.** What Confederate major general had to be released from arrest in order to lead his troops in mid-September 1862?

**A.** Ambrose P. Hill (*b*. Virginia).

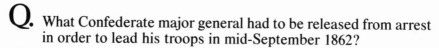

**Q.** Who, more than any other individual, brought about the first real battle, at Manassas, Virginia?

**A.** Abraham Lincoln, against opposition of his generals.

**Q.** Overwhelmed by superior forces at Rich Mountain, Virginia, on July 11, 1861, what Confederate officer manned his only cannon alone before falling wounded?

**A.** Capt. Julius Adolph de Lagnel (*b*. New Jersey).

**Q.** What was the prewar vocation of colorful and controversial Maj. Gen. Edward Ferrero, U.S.A.?

**A.** Dance instructor to West Point cadets.

**Q.** What was the chief booty captured by Confederates under Wade Hampton at Coggins' Point, Virginia, September 16, 1864?

**A.** Nearly 2,500 head of cattle, making a seven-mile column.

**Q.** What plot was detailed in the notorious Dahlgren papers found on the body of Union colonel Ulric Dahlgren when he was killed at King and Queen Court House, March 2, 1864?

**A.** Murder of Jefferson Davis and his cabinet.

**Q.** Who was Robert E. Lee's father?

**A.** Henry ("Lighthouse Harry") Lee, a cavalry hero of the American Revolution.

**Q.** Who was the first person to direct artillery fire for an army via aerial reconnaissance?

**A.** Balloonist Thaddeus Lowe, U.S.A., September 24, 1861.

———◆———

**Q.** In what battle did A. P. Hill, C.S.A., have three horses shot from under him within hours?

**A.** Second Bull Run.

———◆———

**Q.** Where did Brig. Gen. Richard S. Ewell, C.S.A., lose a leg to a minié ball?

**A.** At Groveton, Virginia, August 28, 1862.

———◆———

**Q.** Where did the largest cavalry engagement of the war take place?

**A.** Brandy Station, Virginia, June 9, 1863.

———◆———

**Q.** What unit was selected in advance to take the second assault line at The Crater, Petersburg, Virginia, July 30, 1864?

**A.** A black brigade led by Brig. Gen. Edward Ferrero.

———◆———

**Q.** With rations scarce, what foods were especially important to Stonewall Jackson's men in August 1862?

**A.** Beef on the hoof and green corn pulled from fields.

———◆———

**Q.** What Confederate group performed a famed reconnaissance mission, riding one hundred miles around 100,000 Federal troops with the loss of only one man?

**A.** Jeb Stuart's 1,200 cavalrymen in the ride around McClellan, June 12–16, 1862.

[BATTLES AND LEADERS OF THE CIVIL WAR]

As a reward for his great victory at Island No. 10 in the Mississippi River, Brig. Gen. John Pope was called east and promoted. Notoriously unable to get along with his commanders, Pope was removed by Abraham Lincoln from the Army of the Potomac after he had been in command less than three months. Historians usually say that when Lincoln found Grant, he so trusted him that he gave him a free hand. Perhaps. But it is also possible that the president's worries about losing the upcoming election of 1864 kept him so busy he did not have time to deal with Grant as he had with Pope and half a dozen others.

**Q.** What triggered the quarrel between John B. Hood and Nathan G. Evans, C.S.A., that led to Hood's arrest for insubordination?

**A.** Evans laid claim to ambulances captured by Hood.

◆

**Q.** What Confederate led an epochal raid into western Virginia in the spring of 1863, which almost reached the Ohio River?

**A.** Brig. Gen. William E. ("Grumble") Jones (*b*. Virginia).

◆

**Q.** What percentage of its men did the Second Wisconsin lose at Gettysburg on day one of the battle?

**A.** 77 percent.

◆

**Q.** What Confederate partisan raider often disguised his men as Federals or civilians when he raided the Shenandoah Valley in 1862?

**A.** Maj. Harry Gilmor (*b*. Maryland).

**Q.** In lieu of giving medals, the Confederate Congress recognized valor or service in what way?

**A.** Passing resolutions called Thanks of Congress.

---

**Q.** In what battle did the charging troops of Winfield Scott Featherstone, C.S.A., push their foes back so they fell to their deaths over a steep cliff?

**A.** Ball's Bluff, Virginia, October 1861.

---

**Q.** At bloody Antietam, how many Federal and Confederate troops were engaged?

**A.** 87,000 Federals; 40,000-plus Confederates.

---

**Q.** During heavy fighting early in the war, how did men under Stonewall Jackson know friends from foes?

**A.** Jackson ordered his troop to tie strips of white cloth around their hats.

---

**Q.** Repercussions from the Union debacle at Ball's Bluff, caused by the military ineptness of Lincoln's political friend Col. Edward Baker, resulted in what general being made the scapegoat and his career ruined?

**A.** Brig. Gen. Charles P. Stone.

---

**Q.** At what site was salt destroyed in enormous quantities by Union cavalrymen under Gen. George Stoneman?

**A.** Saltville, Virginia, December 1864.

---

**Q.** As the armies moved toward Sharpsburg, Maryland, in September 1862, by what margin was Lee's strength overestimated?

**A.** 500 percent.

Q. At Gettysburg, what Confederate voiced opposition to the eleven-brigade charge led by George E. Pickett?

A. James Longstreet, senior lieutenant general of the C.S.A.

◆

Q. What shortage often reduced the effectiveness of C.S.A. horses and mules?

A. Lack of metal shoes.

◆

Q. When Robert E. Lee's hands were severely injured, how did he stay on his horse, Traveller?

A. He didn't; he rode in an ambulance.

◆

Q. What men claimed, probably truthfully, often to have slept in their saddles?

A. Cavalrymen under J. E. B. Stuart, C.S.A.

◆

Q. Brig. Gen. John Gibbon's Iron Brigade of the West, the only all-western brigade in the Army of the Potomac, were distinguished by unusual headgear that gave them what other nickname?

A. Black Hat Brigade, for their tall black felt hats.

◆

Q. Approximately how many men did Ambrose Burnside, U.S.A., command in November 1862?

A. 250,000: 60 percent in the field, 40 percent defending Washington.

◆

Q. In 1863, draft riots in what northern city protested the passage of the first national conscription act?

A. New York, which contained many southern sympathizers.

The spot where Lee surrendered is among the best-preserved of Civil War sites, a few miles from Farmville, Virginia. Substantially more troops were involved when Joseph E. Johnston decided to come to terms with William T. Sherman. Their initial meeting was in the yard of the James Bennett home at Durham's Station, North Carolina, just west of present-day Durham. Despite the magnitude of events taking place in the tiny farm community, the Bennett home has not received a tiny fraction of the loving care bestowed upon the McLean House, Appomattox.

**Q.** What Union officer's life was saved at Ball's Bluff, Virginia, in October 21, 1861, when a button deflected a rifle ball?

**A.** Col. (later Brig. Gen.) Charles Devens, Jr. (*b.* Massachusetts).

———◆———

**Q.** What percentage of the 9,400 Federals wounded at Antietam were taken to improvised hospitals?

**A.** Nearly 90 percent.

**Q.** At least 50,000 bushels of what scarce commodity were destroyed by Federal troops in December 1864?

**A.** Salt.

———◆———

**Q.** In April 1863, the U. S. Department of War created what special corps made up of soldiers who had been wounded?

**A.** The Invalid Corps, which helped quell the Draft Riot in New York City.

———◆———

**Q.** What Shenandoah Valley town may have set a record by changing hands at least seventy times in four years?

**A.** Winchester, Virginia.

———◆———

**Q.** What percentage of the 490 members of the New York Zouaves were casualties at Groveton, Virginia, in August 1862?

**A.** 71 percent: 124 dead, 223 wounded.

———◆———

**Q.** What battle caused John Pope, U.S.A., to become discredited as a strategist and commander?

**A.** Second Bull Run.

———◆———

**Q.** Some military analysts consider what campaign to be Robert E. Lee's greatest achievement, unrivaled by that of any other American?

**A.** Chancellorsville.

———◆———

**Q.** What principal figure in the Saltville, Virginia, murder of Federal black troops was later captured and hanged for the crime?

**A.** Capt. Champ Ferguson, head of a body of irregulars.

**Q.** What commander, who wrote daily letters to his wife, had handwriting called "spidery"?

**A.** Stonewall Jackson.

---

**Q.** How did infantry get across White's Ford, south of Fredericksburg, Virginia, in September 1862?

**A.** They waded, with those having shoes taking them off.

---

**Q.** What C.S.A. leader, without previous military training, lost two regiments in a railroad cut at Gettysburg?

**A.** Brig. Gen. Joseph R. Davis, of the Tenth Mississippi.

---

**Q.** What commander often inspected gun crews while wearing carpet slippers?

**A.** James Longstreet, the senior lieutenant general of the C.S.A.

---

**Q.** After losing five thousand men in a day but claiming a win, what general wrote that "God has been kind this day"?

**A.** Stonewall Jackson.

---

**Q.** Where did J. E. B. Stuart's C.S.A. raiders capture the hat, cloak, and dress uniform of John Pope, U.S.A.?

**A.** Catlett's Station, Virginia, August 1862.

---

**Q.** What did U. S. Grant call the biggest explosion of the war, which created The Crater at Petersburg?

**A.** "A stupendous failure."

---

**Q.** Why did Robert E. Lee defend Petersburg, Virginia, against an unrelenting ten-month siege?

**A.** It was the rail center of the entire region.

**Q.** What Confederate stratagem at Drewry's Bluff, Virginia, saved the city of Richmond from capture by Union ships on May 15, 1862?

**A.** Weighted hulks were sunk in the James River as obstructions.

———◆———

**Q.** After the disaster of Pickett's Charge at Gettysburg, upon whom did Robert E. Lee place the blame?

**A.** Himself, reputedly saying, "It's all my fault."

———◆———

**Q.** Why did Confederate authorities have Maj. Harry Gilmor, leader of a partisan raiding group, face court martial?

**A.** His men were said to have robbed a train and bothered women.

———◆———

**Q.** What area was called by newspapers and military leaders the "bloodiest region in America"?

**A.** The one-hundred-mile stretch between Washington and Richmond.

———◆———

**Q.** During the fearful Seven Days' Campaign in Virginia, what were Federal and Confederate losses?

**A.** Federal, 15,849; Confederate, 20,141.

———◆———

**Q.** According to legend, where did soldiers in blue and gray enact an unofficial truce during the second night at Gettysburg?

**A.** Spangler's Spring, sharing the cool water.

———◆———

**Q.** On his June 1862 ride around McClellan's army, why did J. E. B. Stuart, C.S.A., especially dread the possibility of meeting Brig. Gen. Philip St. George Cooke?

**A.** Blue-clad Cooke was his father-in-law.

*Within hours after Johnston and Sherman agreed upon terms, the Bennett house and surrounding buildings were stacked head-high with Confederate weapons. Sherman's terms were so generous that he was called to Washington and rebuked, and Congress rewrote the Union-Confederate agreement.*

Q. What was the length of the record-breaking pontoon bridge thrown across the James River by Federals in June 1864?

A. 2,100 feet, formed by 101 pontoons.

◆

Q. Civilian balloonist Thaddeus Lowe had his fame boosted in a nine-hour flight in 1861 that traveled what distance?

A. 900 miles (from Cincinatti, Ohio, to Unionville, South Carolina).

◆

Q. The battle known to Confederates as Beaver Dam Creek or Ellerson's Mill was called by what name in the Union?

A. Mechanicsville, Virginia.

**Q.** What Union regiment suffered the greatest percentage of casualties at First Bull Run?

**A.** The First Minnesota Infantry, 180 casualties in one day.

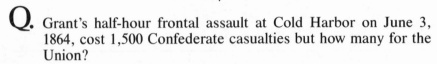

**Q.** Grant's half-hour frontal assault at Cold Harbor on June 3, 1864, cost 1,500 Confederate casualties but how many for the Union?

**A.** About 7,000.

**Q.** What battle site near Petersburg was identified by Federals as a farm, and as a church by Confederates?

**A.** Peebles' Farm or Poplar Spring Church.

**Q.** During the long Peninsula campaign of 1862, about how many troops did Lee assign to the defense of Richmond?

**A.** Twenty-five thousand.

**Q.** What was the longest uninterrupted campaign of the entire Civil War conflict?

**A.** The Petersburg, Virginia, campaign, June 15, 1864–April 3, 1865.

**Q.** The Petersburg campaign cost how many Confederate and Federal casualties?

**A.** Confederate, 28,000; Union 42,000.

# 11

# War in the South and West

**Q.** Although General Rosecrans reported a Union victory at Stone's River, Tennessee, how did his casualties compare with those of the Confederates?

**A.** Union: 13,200; Confederate 10,266.

———◆———

**Q.** What northern general, threatened with being relieved of his command, was described to President Lincoln in 1861 as "a drunken wooden-headed tanner"?

**A.** U. S. Grant.

———◆———

**Q.** In what state did the engagement of Coffeeville take place?

**A.** Mississippi, April 4, 1862.

———◆———

**Q.** From what site was the last large Federal land campaign launched?

**A.** Fort Morgan, Alabama.

———◆———

**Q.** Although they fought only skirmishes, what troops made a heroic march in 1862 across mountains and desert to secure the Arizona Territory for the Union?

**A.** The Column from California under Col. James H. Carlton.

**Q.** Prior to the Civil War, what was the military experience of Lt. Richard Dowling, whose men were decorated for Sabine Pass?

**A.** None; before the war he was a Houston, Texas, saloon keeper.

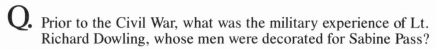

**Q.** In what engagement was a Confederate retreat order misinterpreted by Franz Sigel, U.S.A., who feared a flanking attack, so launched a retreat of his own?

**A.** At Carthage, Missouri, July 7, 1861.

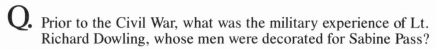

**Q.** When Indian fighter John R. Baylor recruited 1,000 fellow Texans in spring 1861, actually to secure the New Mexico Territory for the Confederacy, what did he say his mission was?

**A.** A buffalo hunt.

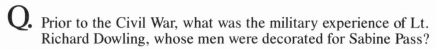

**Q.** Anticipating withdrawal from Kentucky, Braxton Bragg, C.S.A., ordered about how many rations collected?

**A.** More than 300,000.

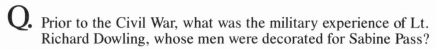

**Q.** Sometimes referred to as the battle of Guntown or Tishomingo Creek, what did the Federals call an April 1864 engagement in Mississippi?

**A.** Brice's Cross Roads.

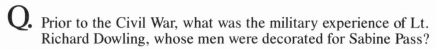

**Q.** What Pennsylvania native, renowned as the "defender of Vicksburg," surrendered the city to Grant July 4, 1863?

**A.** Lt. Gen. John Clifford Pemberton.

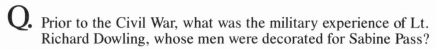

**Q.** On the dismal retreat from Nashville in 1864, soldiers of the Army of Tennessee parodied what popular song?

**A.** "The Yellow Rose of Texas" ("But the gallant Hood of Texas/Played hell in Tennessee").

Q. Civilians lined the steps of what state capitol—and surrounding hills—to watch what battle on December 16, 1864?

A. Tennessee, at Nashville.

———◆———

Q. Who was the highest-ranking officer of the war treated as having been absent without official leave?

A. P. T. G. Beauregard (hampered by illness).

---

### A Commander to Remember

Pierre Gustave Toutant Beauregard is best remembered for having directed the Confederate attack upon Fort Sumter, commanded by his one-time artillery instructor, Robert Anderson. Not a one-shot celebrity, Beauregard also holds an all-time record as superintendent at West Point. His tenure in the post was the shortest ever, exactly eight days, beginning January 23, 1861.

---

Q. At Franklin, Tennessee, what open-field distance had to be crossed for the attack ordered by John B. Hood, C.S.A.?

A. Approximately two miles.

———◆———

Q. In Federally-occupied New Orleans, who had a citizen hanged for wearing a fragment of a torn-up U.S. flag?

A. Benjamin F. Butler, widely known as "Beast Butler".

———◆———

Q. What Confederate cavalryman sometimes demanded surrender as "Brigadier General of Cavalry, C.S.A"?

A. Nathan Bedford Forrest.

Q. What river was used by Federal forces in a combined land and naval foray into Texas in May 1864?

A. The Red River.

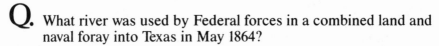

Q. Where did Rear Adm. David G. Farragut, U.S.N., place a garrison of 3,200 in late July 1862?

A. Baton Rouge, Louisiana.

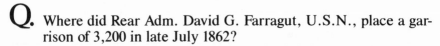

Q. What commander, made a major general at Shiloh, wore rose-colored kid gloves and shirts with frilled fronts?

A. Thomas Carmichael Hindman, C.S.A. (*b*. Tennessee).

Q. After Pea Ridge, Arkansas, who succeeded Lew Wallace as the youngest Union general?

A. Francis J. Herron (*b*. February 17, 1837, Pennsylvania).

Q. How many Confederates were transported on the Montgomery and West Point Railroad from Tupelo, Mississippi, to Chattanooga, in July 1861?

A. Four divisions, more than 31,000 men.

Q. Who was the first officer to be killed west of the Mississippi?

A. Brig. Gen. Nathaniel Lyon of the Missouri State Militia, killed August 10, 1861, at Wilson's Creek, Missouri.

Q. At Arkansas Post (Fort Hindman), January 10–11, 1863, in addition to large amounts of materiel and supplies, how many Confederate prisoners were taken, the largest number since Island No. 10?

A. 4,792.

**Q.** Who roundly denounced destruction at Napoleon, Louisiana, during the first month of 1863?

**A.** William Tecumseh Sherman, U.S.A.

---

**Q.** What city in northern Georgia, not far from the Western and Atlantic Railroad, had a cannon factory?

**A.** Rome, Georgia (target of Streight's Raid).

---

**Q.** What creative ruse did Nathan Bedford Forrest employ to cause Union colonel Abel Streight to surrender at Lawrence, Alabama, on May 3, 1863?

**A.** Calling out orders to imaginary units, Forrest kept moving one section of artillery in circles, so Streight thought he was surrounded.

---

**Q.** What Union objective was described by Gen. Henry Halleck, U.S.A., as "more important than twenty Richmonds"?

**A.** Control of the Mississippi River.

---

**Q.** After Stone's River, Tennessee, what new name was given to the area known as the Round Forest?

**A.** Hell's Half-Acre.

---

**Q.** What Confederate was relieved of his command by Jefferson Davis because he was considered having been A.W.O.L.?

**A.** P. T. G. Beauregard, June 1862.

---

**Q.** What was a major motive for Sherman's attempt to drive Nathan B. Forrest from northern Mississippi in June 1864?

**A.** To prevent Forrest from cutting the Nashville and Chattanooga Railroad.

[ARTIST UNKNOWN]

*When Ulysses S. Grant left Galena, Illinois, it is likely that his wife was glad to see a perennial failure get a regular job by donning a uniform. Grant scored the first big Federal victory at Fort Donelson but found it impossible to stay out of trouble. Demoted for insubordination, he was restored to command just in time to score a major victory on the second day at Shiloh. Although Shiloh did not mark the end of his troubles with superiors, his fighting in the South and the West persuaded Abraham Lincoln to place him in charge of the entire Union operation.*

**Q.** At what site were Confederates accused of having driven wagons over wounded black soldiers?

**A.** Poison Springs, Arkansas, April 18, 1864.

◆

**Q.** What Kentucky town was a major Confederate source of the all-important, and very scarce, salt used to preserve meat rations?

**A.** Barbourville.

**Q.** Capture of what Confederate center was the cause for "a wing-dinger of a July 4th celebration" in 1863?

**A.** Vicksburg, Mississippi.

---

**Q.** Near what city did about 16,000 Confederates keep 55,000 Federals at bay in October 1862?

**A.** Perryville, Kentucky.

---

**Q.** How did animals aid the enemy during Union colonel Abel Streight's raid into northern Alabama in the spring of 1863?

**A.** Braying of their mules betrayed their location.

---

**Q.** The first "sanitary fair" to raise money for the benefit of Union soldiers was held in what city?

**A.** Chicago, fall 1863.

---

**Q.** Who were Halleck Tustenuggee and Opothleyahola?

**A.** Pro-Union leaders of Creek and Seminole Indians who fought for the Union in Indian Territory.

---

**Q.** What Confederate commander who wore a French-made cork leg always carried a spare on his saddle?

**A.** Maj. Gen. John B. Hood.

---

**Q.** What woman physician, working as an assistant surgeon in Kentucky and Tennessee, was awarded the Medal of Honor?

**A.** Mary Edwards Walker.

---

**Q.** Ordered to reduce Vicksburg, Mississippi, David G. Farragut bombarded the city with Federal naval guns for how long?

**A.** Sixty-seven days, with no success (the summer of 1862).

**Q.** What Charleston shipping and banking firm had an English subsidiary that acted as the unofficial depository for Confederate finance overseas?

**A.** John Fraser and Company.

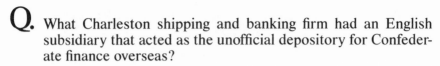

**Q.** When John H. Morgan, C.S.A., was married at Murfreesboro, Tennessee, in December 1862, what did the clergyman wear?

**A.** Vestments of an Episcopal bishop over the uniform of a Confederate lieutenant general (Leonidas Polk).

**Q.** When 4,500 Confederates attacked Union positions late on January 2, 1863, at Murfreesboro, Tennessee, what drove them back?

**A.** Concerted fire of fifty-seven cannon in Federal field batteries.

**Q.** What Confederate commander kept his army in the field for six weeks after the surrender at Appomattox?

**A.** Lt. Gen. E. Kirby Smith, commander of the Trans-Mississippi Department.

**Q.** Early in the war, what force held the all-important St. Louis arsenal?

**A.** Confederate partisans.

**Q.** What regiments of the regular U.S. Army served only in the West?

**A.** Thirteenth, Fifteenth, Sixteenth, Eighteenth, and Nineteenth regiments.

**Q.** Where did Kentucky officials flee when it became apparent that Confederate forces would take Frankfort?

**A.** Louisville.

**Dr. Mary Walker**
Army Surgeon

Medal of Honor
USA 2Oc

[U.S. POSTAL SERVICE]

*Mary E. Walker, M.D., was initially refused an appointment in Union armies. She wangled a place as assistant surgeon from Gen. George Thomas and served on battlefields in Kentucky and Tennessee. In 1917 Congress revoked the Medal of Honor awarded to her in 1865 and asked for its return, which she refused to do; she died still retaining it. As sketched by an unknown artist, she looks as though she could hold her own with the fellows in the ranks. When depicted on a twenty-cent stamp by the U.S. Postal Service, she was made to look so demure and feminine that no one would have picked her as having been the only female army surgeon of the war.*

**Q.** How many casualties were there during the first day of fierce fighting at Murfreesboro, Tennessee, on December 31, 1862?

**A.** About 25,000.

———◆———

**Q.** What riverboat led the Federal flotilla of rams in the battle of Memphis?

**A.** The USS *Queen of the West.*

———◆———

**Q.** What was the "white gold" that Confederate leaders hoped to use as a diplomatic bargaining tool with European governments?

**A.** Cotton, but supplies from Egypt, India, and Brazil soon replaced that from the Deep South in foreign markets.

**Q.** Where in Kansas did bushwhackers led by irregular Confederate William C. Quantrill massacre numerous Federals?

**A.** Baxter Springs, Kansas, October 6, 1863.

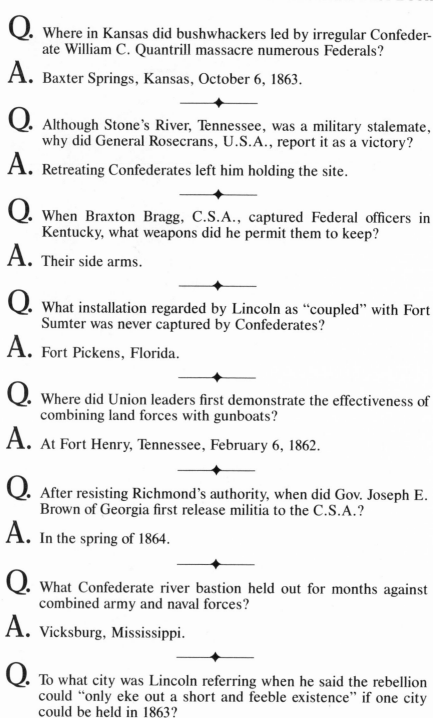

**Q.** Although Stone's River, Tennessee, was a military stalemate, why did General Rosecrans, U.S.A., report it as a victory?

**A.** Retreating Confederates left him holding the site.

**Q.** When Braxton Bragg, C.S.A., captured Federal officers in Kentucky, what weapons did he permit them to keep?

**A.** Their side arms.

**Q.** What installation regarded by Lincoln as "coupled" with Fort Sumter was never captured by Confederates?

**A.** Fort Pickens, Florida.

**Q.** Where did Union leaders first demonstrate the effectiveness of combining land forces with gunboats?

**A.** At Fort Henry, Tennessee, February 6, 1862.

**Q.** After resisting Richmond's authority, when did Gov. Joseph E. Brown of Georgia first release militia to the C.S.A.?

**A.** In the spring of 1864.

**Q.** What Confederate river bastion held out for months against combined army and naval forces?

**A.** Vicksburg, Mississippi.

**Q.** To what city was Lincoln referring when he said the rebellion could "only eke out a short and feeble existence" if one city could be held in 1863?

**A.** Chattanooga, Tennessee.

**Q.** The capture of what rail center is widely credited with bringing about Lincoln's reelection in 1864?

**A.** Atlanta.

---

**Q.** During skirmishing in Kentucky, what C.S.A. commander rode into the lines of the Twenty-seventh Indiana at twilight, ordered a cease fire, then rode away unrecognized?

**A.** The Bishop-general Leonidas Polk.

---

**Q.** What sole Federal victory was so smashing that the opposing C.S.A. army was virtually destroyed?

**A.** Nashville, Tennessee, December 15–16, 1864.

---

**Q.** How many men joined the First Kansas Colored Volunteers?

**A.** More than five hundred, in a state with few black residents.

---

**Q.** What fort had been built by the U. S. government to protect Mobile Bay?

**A.** Fort Morgan, named for Daniel Morgan.

---

**Q.** When did federal authorities first lose control of Fort Morgan?

**A.** January 5, 1861, six days before Alabama seceded.

---

**Q.** What was the last significant Confederate fortification on the Atlantic coast to hold out against Union forces?

**A.** Fort Fisher, North Carolina, captured December 17, 1864.

---

**Q.** What famous steamer, altered into a ram, was captured by Confederates on the Red River on February 5, 1863, and used by them?

**A.** The USS *Queen of the West*.

**Q.** What U.S. naval officer on the upper Mississippi habitually preached when no chaplain was available?

**A.** Andrew H. Foote, later an admiral.

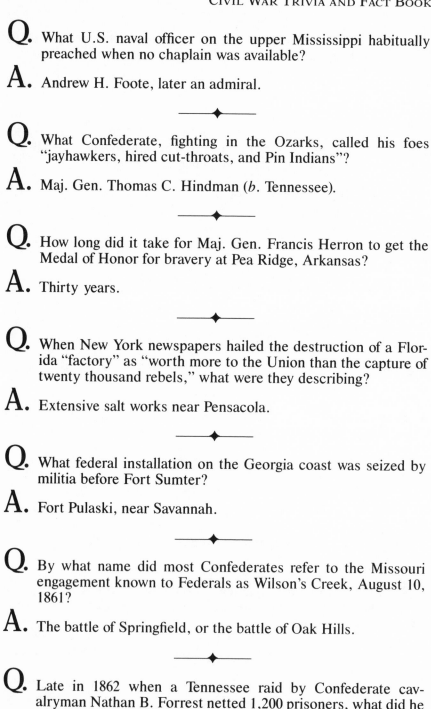

**Q.** What Confederate, fighting in the Ozarks, called his foes "jayhawkers, hired cut-throats, and Pin Indians"?

**A.** Maj. Gen. Thomas C. Hindman (*b.* Tennessee).

**Q.** How long did it take for Maj. Gen. Francis Herron to get the Medal of Honor for bravery at Pea Ridge, Arkansas?

**A.** Thirty years.

**Q.** When New York newspapers hailed the destruction of a Florida "factory" as "worth more to the Union than the capture of twenty thousand rebels," what were they describing?

**A.** Extensive salt works near Pensacola.

**Q.** What federal installation on the Georgia coast was seized by militia before Fort Sumter?

**A.** Fort Pulaski, near Savannah.

**Q.** By what name did most Confederates refer to the Missouri engagement known to Federals as Wilson's Creek, August 10, 1861?

**A.** The battle of Springfield, or the battle of Oak Hills.

**Q.** Late in 1862 when a Tennessee raid by Confederate cavalryman Nathan B. Forrest netted 1,200 prisoners, what did he do with them?

**A.** Paroled them on the spot, a frequent practice.

**Q.** What was the first Atlantic coast fort of the Confederacy to be surrendered, in August 1861?

**A.** Fort Hatteras, North Carolina.

———◆———

**Q.** At Shiloh, what did members of the C.S.A. Orleans Guard do to their blue uniforms?

**A.** They turned them inside out, to avoid "friendly fire."

———◆———

**Q.** Why was Fort Brooke, Florida, which successfully resisted two Federal attacks after C.S.A. seizure, built in so remote a spot?

**A.** For protection of peaceful Seminoles from other Indian tribes, it was located on Tampa Bay.

———◆———

**Q.** What famous painting depicts Missouri residents being driven from their homes by Union troops?

**A.** "Order No. 11," painted by George Caleb Bingham, in 1868.

———◆———

**Q.** Outlaw William Quantrill and his guerrillas committed a major atrocity at what Kansas town in August 1863?

**A.** Lawrence.

———◆———

**Q.** At what place were men under Nathan B. Forrest, C.S.A., widely accused of murdering about one hundred black soldiers?

**A.** At Fort Pillow, Tennessee, April 12, 1864.

———◆———

**Q.** What nurse, rejected by Dorothea Dix as too young, gave conspicuous service at Andersonville Prison?

**A.** Maria Hall (*b.* District of Columbia).

Q. What was a major cause of overcrowding at Andersonville Prison?

A. Suspension of prisoner exchange.

———◆———

Q. In 1864, the unsuccessful Missouri raid led by what general marked the eve of official Confederate operations beyond the Mississippi?

A. Maj. Gen. Sterling Price.

---

### Grueling Feats

In Missouri, Gen. Nathaniel Lyon called a regiment of volunteers his "Iowa greyhounds" as a token of admiration for their long legs. Early in the war, they set a record probably not matched even by those whom Stonewall Jackson dubbed his "foot cavalry." During one twenty-four-hour period, the Iowa greyhounds marched a little more than forty-eight miles.

———◆———

Brig. Gen. John Hunt Morgan was ordered into Kentucky in early June 1863. Ignoring instructions from Braxton Bragg, he led his cavalry units across the Ohio River on June 7; once on Indiana soil, he turned east toward Ohio. He and a band of more than 300 riders were captured near New Lisbon, Ohio, on July 26. Federal commanders traced movements of the Confederates and found that since crossing "the big river," raiders had spent an average of twenty-one hours per day in the saddle.

---

Q. The Federal capture of what two fortifications cost the C.S.A. western Tennessee?

A. Forts Henry and Donelson.

———◆———

Q. What was the only major southern port still in Confederate hands at the end of the war?

A. Galveston, Texas.

**Q.** Near Poison Springs, Arkansas, 87 white and 117 black Federals died protecting a wagon train containing what commodity?

**A.** Corn, raided from Confederate stores.

———◆———

**Q.** What pro-Southern governor, who was deposed when his state voted to remain in the Union, led his untrained and poorly equipped militia against Nathaniel Lyon's Federals in July 1861?

**A.** Claiborne Jackson of Missouri.

———◆———

**Q.** In what state did the Pon Pon River engagement of July 10, 1863, take place?

**A.** South Carolina.

———◆———

**Q.** What Federal expedition into Arkansas, launched March 23, 1864, was a conspicuous failure?

**A.** Maj. Gen. Frederick Steele's Camden expedition.

———◆———

**Q.** What Union general is credited with driving invading Confederates from the New Mexico Territory?

**A.** Maj. Gen. Edward R. S. Canby (*b.* Kentucky).

———◆———

**Q.** What Confederate general, serving as a U. S. Army engineer before the war, helped design Fort Pulaski, Georgia, and other installations later seized by the C.S.A.?

**A.** Robert E. Lee.

———◆———

**Q.** In February 1861, where in New Mexico Territory did Confederates under Henry H. Sibley score a victory, giving the South hope it might conquer all the Southwest?

**A.** Valverde.

Q. In 1919, when Congress revoked many Medals of Honor previously awarded, what Civil War woman recipient refused to return hers six days before her death?

A. Mary Walker, M.D., whose medal was reinstated in 1977.

◆

Q. What naval captain, later a rear admiral, was head of the Union's Blockade Strategy Board organizing the blockade and planning amphibious operations?

A. Samuel F. Du Pont.

◆

Q. What was the first and only target of the monitor, USS *Catskill*, in March 1862?

A. Charleston Harbor, as part of the blockade.

◆

Q. What Confederate guerrilla was charged with having massacred twenty-four Union soldiers at Centralia, Missouri, in September 1864?

A. William ("Bloody Bill") Anderson, a self-styled colonel.

◆

Q. While gunners on Rear Adm. Samuel Du Pont's warships scored about sixty hits on Fort Sumter, how many hits did they receive?

A. At least four hundred.

◆

Q. What route did troops of U. S. Grant follow on his first march toward Vicksburg, Mississippi, in December 1862?

A. Tracks of the Mississippi Central Railroad.

◆

Q. What was the cost of a Union victory over Nathan Bedford Forrest and his troops near Ebenezer Church, Alabama, on April 1, 1865?

A. A dozen men in blue were killed, forty wounded.

*Cherokee warriors who fought at Pea Ridge, Arkansas, were only a few of the native Americans who espoused the cause of the C.S.A. Old Indian hand Gen. Albert Pike accepted Jefferson Davis's invitation to recruit as many as possible. After making an October 1861 treaty with Chief John Ross of the Cherokee Nation, Pike raised an estimated 3,500 Indians to fight the Yankees. None of the native volunteers is known to have worn Confederate gray, however; they needed no uniforms to be identified. Only a handful of tribesmen enlisted in Union armies.*

**Q.** After reaching the Atlantic Ocean, what was Sherman's initial plan for moving his army from the Georgia coast to join Grant's forces?

**A.** He expected to use Federal transport ships.

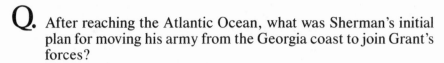

**Q.** Why did Sherman's March to the Sea and his ensuing Carolinas campaign mark him as one of the first "modern" military leaders?

**A.** They embodied total warfare massive destruction, calculated to bring victory.

**Q.** What was the duration of the March to the Sea?

**A.** Twenty-six days: November 15–December 10, 1864.

**Q.** With Florida far from scenes of major conflict, when was the Union Department of Florida created?

**A.** April 13, 1861, one day after Fort Sumter, by Winfield Scott.

**Q.** What was the largest cavalry engagement of the war?

**A.** Brandy Station, Virginia, June 9, 1863.

**Q.** Who led the eight thousand men who reduced Fort Fisher, North Carolina, in December 1864, "slamming the only coastal door of the C.S.A."?

**A.** Brig. Gen. Alfred H. Terry (*b*. Connecticut).

**Q.** After five men led by C.S.A. guerrilla William C. Quantrill were accidentally killed while locked up in a Kansas City warehouse, how did Quantrill get revenge?

**A.** He raided and sacked Lawrence, Kansas, killing 150.

**Q.** Of the 250 blacks who fought at Fort Pillow, Tennessee, on March 12, 1864, how many died that day?

**A.** Approximately two hundred: abolitionists called it a massacre.

———◆———

**Q.** Where did Sherman meet armed resistance during his March to the Sea?

**A.** At Griswoldville, Georgia, November 22, 1864.

———◆———

**Q.** At what western Virginia site, in July 1861, did George B. McClellan become an instant celebrity?

**A.** At Rich Mountain (now in West Virginia).

———◆———

**Q.** When James H. Wilson, U.S.A., demanded the surrender of Macon, Georgia, who met him to ask for a truce?

**A.** Wilson's West Point classmate, Felix H. Robertson.

———◆———

**Q.** Where "in the West" did an August 26, 1863, engagement take place at a now-famous resort?

**A.** White Sulphur Springs, West Virginia.

———◆———

**Q.** What was the Union/C.S.A. casualty ratio at Port Hudson, Louisiana, May 27, 1863?

**A.** Approximately 8:1; Union: 2,000; C.S.A.: 265.

———◆———

**Q.** In December 1862, how long did it take Federals to march 110 miles to Fayetteville, Arkansas?

**A.** Three days (2,000 cavalry and 4,000 infantry).

———◆———

**Q.** The death of what distinguished full general at Shiloh was a great blow to the Confederate command?

**A.** Albert Sidney Johnston.

Q. During the Red River campaign, how did Federals get ships of a combined land/river operation through low water at Alexandria, Louisiana?

A. By building a dam to raise the water level from three to seven feet.

———————◆———————

Q. In daring raids in West Virginia, what Confederate cavalryman captured prisoners, horses, arms, and all-important rations?

A. Maj. Gen. Thomas L. Rosser.

---

### A New Use for Mexican Dollars

At Sabine Pass, Texas, forty-four members of the Davis Guard had just six pieces of artillery available to confront the onslaught of four Federal gunboats and seven troop transports on September 9, 1863. Incredibly, Confederate gunners turned back the invasion flotilla—then accepted the surrender of more than 400 soldiers.

For this feat, Lt. Richard W. Dowling and his guardsmen received the only Confederate medal for valor awarded in the metal-scarce South. Their trophy was a smoothed-down Mexican silver dollar engraved on one side with the place and date of battle. A variety of crudely produced initials and emblems on the reverse side of the coin served to make each medal personal and individual.

---

Q. What Federal cavalry unit at no time served at a point east of the Mississippi River?

A. The Third Cavalry and most members of the Fourth.

———————◆———————

Q. Who commanded the largest mounted force under a single leader in the history of North America?

A. Brig. Gen. James H. Wilson, U.S.A. (in Alabama and Georgia).

*Few men in Federal uniforms gave Richmond, Virginia, so much trouble as did the Hon. Joseph E. Brown. As wartime governor of Georgia, he stuck to states' rights views that had led to secession. Brown refused to turn units of the Georgia militia over to C.S.A. military leaders and manufactured and stored great quantities of clothing and ammunition, strictly for use within the state. After Sherman reached the heart of Georgia, Brown even tried to negotiate terms of peace with him instead of leaving negotiations to authorities in Richmond.*

[GEORGIA DEPARTMENT OF ARCHIVES AND HISTORY]

**Q.** The fall of what city on April 2, 1865, spelled "the collapse of the interior of the C.S.A."?

**A.** Selma, Alabama.

———◆———

**Q.** What Confederate brigade that fought mostly in the west used red sumac on their hats as an identifying symbol?

**A.** The Iron Brigade of the West under Col. Joseph O. Shelby.

———◆———

**Q.** Approximately how many miles were covered by Shelby's infantrymen in their forty-one-day march in the West?

**A.** More than thirty-six miles per day, for a total of 1,500 miles.

———◆———

**Q.** At what site did then-inconspicuous Col. Philip Henry Sheridan, U.S.A., begin to attract Lincoln's attention?

**A.** At Booneville, Mississippi, July 1, 1862.

# 12

# War on the Water: Salt and Fresh

**Q.** The loyalty of what Union naval officer was questioned because of his southern roots?

**A.** Adm. David G. Farragut, who was born in Tennessee.

———◆———

**Q.** In what waters did David Farragut, U.S.N., reputedly cry, "Damn the torpedoes! Full steam ahead!"?

**A.** Mobile Bay, Alabama, August 5, 1864.

———◆———

**Q.** What Confederate ironclad dueled with Farragut's flagship, the USS *Hartford*, in Mobile Bay?

**A.** The CSS *Tennessee*.

———◆———

**Q.** Jeering Confederates aboard what southern vessel called the USS *Monitor* the "tin can on a shingle"?

**A.** The CSS *Virginia*.

———◆———

**Q.** What was the result of the famed duel between the *Monitor* and the *Virginia (Merrimack)*?

**A.** A four-hour fight ended in a draw.

*No one knew precisely how many men crowded aboard the USS* Sultana *on April 27, 1865. One estimate said there were about 1,900 troops plus 75 civilians, 80 members of the crew, 62 horses and mules, and "somewhat more than 100 hogs." Overworked boilers exploded and took to the bottom at least 1,650 men recently paroled from southern prisons. Far the most deadly disaster of the era, it received scant coverage; folk were too busy rejoicing that the war was over to give more than passing attention to "another tragedy on the Mississippi."*

Q. When the two-million-dollar fleet of David Porter, U.S.N., was stranded in the Red River, how long did it take to raise the water level by means of wing dams?

A. Fourteen days, April 30–May 13, 1864.

———◆———

Q. What Confederate vessel was regarded as a prize of war by the U.S. government even though it was owned by an Englishman when a Federal ship captured it?

A. CSS *Georgia.*

**Q.** What vessels widely used on rivers by both sides were named for an animal?

**A.** Rams, designed to butt holes in enemy ships.

———◆———

**Q.** The side-wheel steam vessel USS *Red Rover* was used for what purpose?

**A.** Hospital ship attached to the Mississippi Squadron.

---

### A Trio of "Class L" Ironclads

Though the category was never official, just three ironclads qualified to be listed as "Ironclads, Class L." Two cruisers, the CSS *Charleston* and the CSS *Fredericksburg*, were only modestly successful. But the 600-ton CSS *Georgia*—converted from the Scottish-owned merchant ship *Japan*—racked up a record by taking nine prizes.

Each of the three warships was purchased with money raised by raffles, auctions, concerts, and fairs sponsored by Ladies' Gunboat societies throughout the South.

---

**Q.** What name of an insect was given to a flotilla of light-draft stern-wheel river vessels?

**A.** The mosquito fleet.

———◆———

**Q.** What early action by Lincoln was considered illegal under international law?

**A.** Blockade of southern ports.

———◆———

**Q.** What forty-nine-year-old member of an outstanding naval family was promoted over eighty senior officers to become acting rear admiral in July 1863?

**A.** David D. Porter, U.S.N. (*b.* Pennsylvania, June 8, 1813).

**Q.** What Confederate warship drew the USS *Hatteras* into a trap by posing as a bark-rigged merchantman?

**A.** The CSS *Alabama* in January 1863, off the Texas coast.

———◆———

**Q.** To what nation did many Northern owners transfer ships' registrations because of C.S.A. raiders?

**A.** England.

———◆———

**Q.** About how many northern-owned ships were flying England's Union Jack at war's end?

**A.** More than 700.

———◆———

**Q.** Who was the first to propose that Union forces gain control of the Mississippi River in order to cut the Confederacy in two?

**A.** Gen. Winfield Scott, U.S. Army.

———◆———

**Q.** During the early months of the war on the Mississippi River, what officer usually commanded a warship?

**A.** An army officer, Union or Confederate.

———◆———

**Q.** What Federal rear admiral was responsible for the Mississippi River operations in 1863?

**A.** David D. Porter.

———◆———

**Q.** When did Federals launch an attack aimed at gaining Pamlico Sound, North Carolina?

**A.** August 1861, sending a fleet of fourteen vessels.

———◆———

**Q.** What South Carolina port between Charleston and Savannah was an early and prime target of Federal expeditions?

**A.** Port Royal.

**Q.** Who was named senior flag officer of the nonexistent Georgia navy in February 1861?

**A.** Josiah Tattnall, who had just resigned from the U.S. Navy.

———◆———

**Q.** What Federal vessel made history by stopping the British Steamer *Trent?*

**A.** The USS *San Jacinto.*

———◆———

**Q.** What passengers were illegally removed from the *Trent* by Capt. Charles Wilkes of the *San Jacinto?*

**A.** C.S.A. commissioners James M. Mason and James Slidell.

———◆———

**Q.** What high-ranking Confederate was "positively delighted" when he learned of the "*Trent* affair"?

**A.** Jefferson Davis.

———◆———

**Q.** How much water was needed to float an Eads-built gunboat, such as those used against Fort Henry?

**A.** Four feet of water.

———◆———

**Q.** What branch of the Federal military machine launched the building of Mississippi River gunboats?

**A.** The U.S. Army.

———◆———

**Q.** What was the usual armament of a work boat converted by the C.S.A. for its "mosquito fleet"?

**A.** One gun, preferably a thirty-two-pound rifle.

———◆———

**Q.** What vessel headed the Federal blockade of Savannah, Georgia, in May 1861?

**A.** The USS *Union*, commanded by John R. Goldsborough.

*The first significant Union naval victory took place at Port Royal, South Carolina, on November 7, 1861. Confederate gunners in Fort Walker poured all the iron they had into the flotilla of warships led by Samuel F. Du Pont. Enemy vessels proved too numerous and too big; after suffering light damage, they drove defenders inland and took possession of one of the finest ports in the South. Today, the region that fell to northern sailors in 1861 is Hilton Head Island, largely owned and part-time inhabited by wealthy newcomers from "Up North."*

Q. Cmdr. Franklin Buchanan, C.S.N., commander of the CSS *Virginia*, had previously held what "first" position in the U.S. Navy?

A. First superintendent of the U.S. Naval Academy, so he was called the "Father of Annapolis."

◆

Q. What two Federal warships were destroyed by the CSS *Virginia* on her trial run on March 8, 1862?

A. The USS *Congress* and the USS *Cumberland*.

**Q.** What executive officer of the USS *Monitor* served under five successive commanders?

**A.** Lt. Samuel Dana Greene (*b*. Maryland).

---

**Q.** What was the first major victory by combined land and water forces of the Union?

**A.** Capture of Island No. 10 in the Mississippi River.

---

**Q.** How many casualties did Federals suffer in the process of capturing Island No. 10 on April 7, 1862?

**A.** None.

---

**Q.** Who directed the six Federal gunboats and eleven mortar boats used in the capture of Island No. 10?

**A.** Andrew H. Foote, U.S.N.

---

**Q.** How many successful voyages made by a C.S.A. blockade runner would pay for the ship?

**A.** Two.

---

**Q.** Because many used smokeless coal and feathered paddles, what were blockade runners called?

**A.** Gray ghosts.

---

**Q.** What C.S.A. installation, named for the river on which it stood, fell to Federal gunboats in April 1862?

**A.** Fort Apalachicola.

---

**Q.** With Fort Apalachicola in Federal hands, what major Mississippi ports soon surrendered to naval guns?

**A.** Biloxi and Pass Christian.

**Q.** At what age did David G. Farragut launch his career in the U.S. Navy as a midshipman?

**A.** At age nine, aboard the USS *Essex*.

---

**Q.** When Confederates built the CSS *Louisiana*, what did they use for armor?

**A.** Double rows of railroad iron.

---

**Q.** Why did experienced commanders have sand and ashes sprinkled around their guns?

**A.** To prevent gunners from slipping in their own blood.

---

**Q.** When Federals launched an April 1862 naval attack upon New Orleans, who was the only man with rank of captain?

**A.** David G. Farragut.

---

**Q.** Because it was on a prolonged voyage and did not know of the surrender, what ship was the last to fly the Confederate flag?

**A.** The CSS *Shenandoah* lowered the colors on November 6, 1865, in Liverpool, England.

---

**Q.** What notable C.S.A. naval officer faced court-martial for his decision to destroy the CSS *Virginia* to thwart its capture?

**A.** Cmdr. Josiah Tattnall.

---

**Q.** What city was headquarters for Josiah Tattnall, commodore of the Confederate navy?

**A.** Savannah, Georgia.

---

**Q.** What admiral invented three kinds of weapons used by the U.S. Navy?

**A.** John A. B. Dahlgren (*b.* Pennsylvania).

*From their unconventional shape and the designer's name, James B. Eads called his armed river boats "Pook turtles." His 512-ton USS* Cairo *could hardly be distinguished from sister craft. After having participated in half a dozen major engagements, this turtle hit two torpedoes— considerably more sophisticated than the earliest "infernal machines" built by Confederates—and went to the bottom in twelve minutes on December 12, 1862.*

Q. What was the largest naval gun made from the Dahlgren design?

A. A twenty-inch smoothbore, but never used.

———◆———

Q. What Federal official succeeded in preventing Confederate purchase of English-built rams, in September 1863?

A. Charles Francis Adams, Sr., minister to England.

**Q.** After having defended Charleston for eighteen months, what was the fate of the CSS *Chicora*?

**A.** Confederates blew her up to prevent her capture.

------◆------

**Q.** Who built the riverboat USS *Cairo* and where?

**A.** James B. Eads, at Mound City, Illinois.

------◆------

**Q.** Where was the famous CSS *Alabama* constructed?

**A.** Liverpool, England.

------◆------

**Q.** What Federal side-wheel steamer was the most powerful gunboat used on western rivers, capable of making two knots per hour going upstream?

**A.** The USS *Choctaw*.

------◆------

**Q.** Because of seniority, what long-time administrator was given command of the ironclad CSS *Virginia*?

**A.** Capt. James Buchanan.

------◆------

**Q.** For what purpose was the CSS *Albemarle* constructed?

**A.** For use in North Carolina coastal shoals.

------◆------

**Q.** For what purpose was the specially designed USS *Alligator* constructed?

**A.** An experimental submarine, it was declared useless.

------◆------

**Q.** What merchantman was converted for use as a Union training vessel for naval recruits?

**A.** The *Ocean Queen*.

**Q.** What Confederate ironclad carrying ten guns and a crew of two hundred was burned to avoid capture?

**A.** The CSS *Arkansas*.

---

**Q.** The USS *Carondelet*, *Tyler*, and *Queen of the West* were all attacked by what Confederate ironclad on July 15, 1862, on the Yazoo River?

**A.** CSS *Arkansas*.

---

**Q.** How many lives were lost in the rapid sinking of the USS *Cairo*, long active in the river fleet?

**A.** None.

---

**Q.** What U.S. naval officer in command of the *Octara* captured a British schooner in June 1863?

**A.** Napoleon Collins.

---

**Q.** How many shots were fired from the Federal monitor *Weehawken* when it destroyed the CSS *Atlanta*?

**A.** Five, of which four were direct hits.

---

**Q.** In what waters was the CSS *Florida* illegally seized and then towed to Hampton Roads?

**A.** Brazilian.

---

**Q.** What was the size of the fleet commanded by David G. Farragut, U.S.N., at Mobile Bay?

**A.** Four ironclad monitors and fourteen wooden warships.

---

**Q.** What U.S. naval officer said that "iron hearts in wooden vessels can get the better of ironclads"?

**A.** Capt. Theordorus Bailey (*b.* New York).

**Q.** What Confederate naval officer was appointed a midshipman at age two?

**A.** Capt. Samuel Barron (*b*. Virginia).

------◆------

**Q.** What Confederate naval captain captured and sank fifty-five ships, more than any other?

**A.** Raphael Semmes of the CSS *Alabama*.

------◆------

**Q.** When the *Alabama* was sunk by the USS *Kearsarge* in French waters, what happened to Captain Semmes?

**A.** He was rescued by the English yacht *Deerhound*.

------◆------

**Q.** In August 1861, a federal force of seven warships and two transports with eight hundred soldiers was dispatched against what North Carolina sites?

**A.** Forts Hatteras and Clark at Hatteras Inlet.

------◆------

**Q.** From what commonplace equipment was the Confederate submarine *H. L. Hunley* built?

**A.** A steam boiler, cut and tapered.

------◆------

**Q.** What provided the power by which the submarine *H. L. Hunley* was propelled?

**A.** Her crew of eight seamen, using hand cranks.

------◆------

**Q.** What Federal gunship blockading Charleston was sunk in the first successful submarine attack?

**A.** The USS *Housatonic*.

------◆------

**Q.** When her Union target went down, what happened to the killer submarine *H. L. Hunley*?

**A.** Her torpedo blast also took her to the bottom.

## By the Light of the Moon

Many a Civil War buff remembers that the moon was full on April 9, 1865, when Lee was forced to surrender to Grant at Appomattox. Many months earlier, on or about September 13, 1862, Robert E. Lee's Special Order No. 191 was lost near Frederick, Maryland, when the moon was full.

◆

If a fellow was superstitious, it might have seemed that a full moon brought no good for the C.S.A. It was shining at its brightest on June 19, 1865, when the CSS *Alabama* was sunk off the coast of France by guns of the USS *Kearsarge*. A full moon bathed the landscape on July 4, 1863, when all-important Vicksburg finally fell before the lengthy Union assault.

Perhaps worst of all, the same phenomenon was due on May 2, 1863, when Confederate troops inflicted mortal wounds upon their leader, Stonewall Jackson. Had the full moon been shining, the landscape would have been brilliantly lighted instead of shrouded in shadows. On this evening, the moon was a few hours too late in making its appearance.

Q. In addition to the USS *Housatonic*, what Union vessel was destroyed by Confederate torpedoes?

A. The USS *Cairo*, in the Mississippi River on December 5, 1862.

◆

Q. When did a Union fleet play a major role in the surrender of the largest city in the C.S.A.?

A. In April 1862, New Orleans.

◆

Q. What wooden Union steamboat destroyed the Southern flagship *Sea Bird* on February 10, 1862?

A. The USS *Commodore Perry* (only 143 feet long).

**Q.** What Union riverboat accidentally rammed the USS *Conestoga* March 8, 1864, sending her to the bottom?

**A.** The USS *General Sterling Price*.

---◆---

**Q.** What Union side-wheel steamer was named for James Buchanan's niece, who was his White House hostess?

**A.** The USS *Harriet Lane*.

---◆---

**Q.** What U.S. Navy officer, serving under his adopted brother David Farragut, commanded the flotilla that won the impressive victory causing the capitulation of New Orleans?

**A.** Cmdr. David D. Porter.

---◆---

**Q.** Where was the USS *Harriet Lane* to be found on April 12, 1861?

**A.** At Charleston, where she had gone with a load of provisions for the Fort Sumter garrison.

---◆---

**Q.** How many lives were lost when the stricken USS *Conestoga* went down in just four minutes?

**A.** Two.

---◆---

**Q.** What rear admiral commanded the largest fleet assembled up to 1864 for the Federal assault on Fort Fisher, North Carolina?

**A.** David Dixon Porter (*b.* Pennsylvania).

---◆---

**Q.** After the war, what Confederate rear admiral was tried by the U.S. government for treason and piracy?

**A.** Capt. Raphael Semmes, C.S.A. (*b.* Maryland).

Q. What side-wheel steamer, named for a U.S. President, was bought for the Union river fleet in June 1861?

A. The USS *Tyler*.

———◆———

Q. Why did Federal crew members most dislike about the USS *Tyler*?

A. The former president for whom it was named was a Confederate.

———◆———

Q. The merchant ship *Japan*, purchased in Scotland, was renamed for what state by the C.S.A.?

A. Georgia.

———◆———

Q. According to some analysts, what was the most significant single Federal operation of the war?

A. The blockade of southern ports.

———◆———

### Boys Sometimes Weren't Really Boys

At age eighteen, Thomas Jackson of Virginia was about average as a cadet just entering West Point. But his class included one member from Philadelphia named George B. McClellan, who was just fifteen. When they graduated in 1846, Jackson was seventeenth in their class of fifty-nine, and the "tadpole from Pennsylvania" was second.

———◆———

Through the influence of his adoptive father, Cmdr. David D. Porter, David G. Farragut was commissioned as a midshipman at age nine. At age twelve, he was placed in command of a prize vessel captured by Porter.

**Q.** Why was shipment of anthracite coal from northern ports to foreign destinations banned?

**A.** Blockade runners burned it to avoid producing smoke.

———◆———

**Q.** Now in the Louisiana State Museum, what was the prototype submarine built by the C.S.A in 1861–62?

**A.** CSS *Pioneer*.

———◆———

**Q.** Why did the *Pioneer* never see action?

**A.** Before it was ready to use, it was scuttled by Confederates to prevent its capture following the fall of New Orleans.

———◆———

**Q.** What were the most deadly guns normally found on warships built for inland waterways?

**A.** Forty-two-pound rifles (conspicuous on the USS *Carondelet*).

———◆———

**Q.** What Tennessean, while serving as a major general of U.S. volunteers, was promoted to lieutenant commander in the U.S. Navy, later retiring as a rear admiral?

**A.** Samuel Powhatan Carter.

———◆———

**Q.** As a U.S. naval officer before the war, what Confederate naval officer had achieved international fame as the "Pathfinder of the Seas" for his pioneering work in oceanography?

**A.** Matthew Fontaine Maury.

———◆———

**Q.** What Union officer managed to be both a major general and a rear admiral?

**A.** Samuel Powhorton Carter (*b.* Tennessee).

*[ILLUSTRATED LONDON NEWS]*

*British ship builders in Liverpool, England, knew they were working for the C.S.A. when they produced No. 290. At least, that was the verdict of an international tribunal in 1872. Renamed the CSS* Alabama, *the sleek 1,050-ton sailing vessel was equipped with an auxiliary steam engine. Pounded mercilessly by a warship of the U.S. Navy, she sank in French waters. But a postwar arbitration panel awarded the U.S. damages of $15.5 million in gold to compensate for "negligence" shown by the British in filling a Confederate order.*

**Q.** What installation was the target of intense fire from big guns of a Federal flotilla on March 7, 1863?

**A.** Fort Sumter, which withstood the fierce attack.

◆

**Q.** What fast 700-ton steamer was converted by Confederates into a gunboat?

**A.** The *Eastport.*

**Q.** What Confederate ship, ready to go into action, was held in a French port and never sailed?

**A.** The CSS *Rappahannock*, detained by Napoleon III.

---

**Q.** What Confederate cruiser successfully ran the blockade and escaped from Charleston in October 1861?

**A.** The CSS *Nashville*.

---

**Q.** Late in 1862, what special assignment did the C.S.A. give to Matthew Fontaine Maury, who had been head of coast, harbor, and river defenses for the Confederate navy?

**A.** Special envoy to England to buy ships and supplies.

---

**Q.** When Confederate ships came out to meet Union vessels attacking Galveston, how were they shielded?

**A.** With dozens of bales of cotton.

---

**Q.** What flag was flown on vessels of the Confederate navy until May 1863?

**A.** The Stars and Bars.

---

**Q.** What was the first cruiser constructed abroad for the Confederate navy?

**A.** The CSS *Florida*, launched in Liverpool, England, in March 1862.

---

**Q.** Who commanded Union naval forces on the upper Mississippi River after August 1861?

**A.** Andrew H. Foote (*b*. Connecticut).

**Q.** What was the displacement of the USS *Hartford*, Admiral Farrogut's flagship at Mobile Bay?

**A.** 2,900 tons.

---

**Q.** What C.S.A. captain was the Gosport Navy Yard head who was in charge of rebuilding and converting the USS *Merrimack*?

**A.** French Forrest.

---

**Q.** Worth an estimated $1.5 million, what ship was the most valuable prize captured by a Confederate cruiser?

**A.** USS *Jacob Bell*, by the CSS *Florida* in February 1863.

---

**Q.** Who is generally credited with having persuaded Gideon Welles, the U.S. secretary of the navy, to experiment with ironclads?

**A.** Gustavus Vasa Fox (*b*. Massachusetts).

---

**Q.** What black slave, an expert pilot around Charleston Harbor, won his freedom and became a hero by escaping to the Union command?

**A.** Robert Smalls.

---

**Q.** At what age did the future rear admiral David D. Porter, U.S.N., go to sea?

**A.** Ten.

---

**Q.** Who was relieved from command of the USS *Oneida* for failure to destroy the CSS *Florida*?

**A.** Lt. George Henry Preble (*b*. Maine).

**Q.** Of the Confederate privateers, which one was the most successful—and notorious?

**A.** The *Jefferson Davis*.

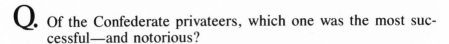

**Q.** What sturdy freighter, made into a Federal ram, was captured by the C.S.A., then recaptured by Federals?

**A.** The *Queen of the West*.

**Q.** As head of the James River Squadron, what commodore gave vital naval support to U. S. Grant's final campaign?

**A.** William Radford (*b*. Virginia).

**Q.** What was the dividing line between the two blockading areas of the U.S. Navy on the east coast?

**A.** The border between North and South Carolina.

**Q.** What double-turreted iron monitor participated in action against Confederate installations on the James River, then at war's end was sold to France where she served until 1903 in coastal defense?

**A.** USS *Onondaga*.

**Q.** Although "The Star-Spangled Banner" was a popular song in the Union during the Civil War, it became the national anthem by act of Congress in what year?

**A.** 1931.

# Bibliography

*American Heritage.* New York, vols. 1–42.

*American History Illustrated.* Harrisburg, Pennsylvania, vol. 1 to date.

Anderson, Bern. *By Sea and by River: The Naval History of the Civil War.* New York, 1962.

*Blue and Gray.* Columbus, Ohio, all volumes.

Boatner, Mark M. III. *The Civil War Dictionary.* New York, 1959.

Bowman, John S., ed. *The Civil War Day by Day.* Greenwich, 1989.

Bruce, Robert V. *Lincoln and the Tools of War.* Indianapolis, 1956.

Buel, Clarence C. and Robert U. Johnson, eds. *Battles and Leaders of the Civil War.* 4 vols. New York, 1888.

Catton, Bruce. *The Coming Fury.* Garden City, 1961.

——————. *Grant Takes Command.* Boston, 1968.

——————. *Mr. Lincoln's Army.* Garden City, 1962.

——————. *Never Call Retreat.* Garden City, 1965.

——————. *A Stillness at Appomattox.* Garden City, 1953.

——————. *The Terrible Swift Sword.* Garden City, 1963.

*Civil War Chronicles.* New York, vol. 1 to date.

*Civil War Times Illustrated.* Harrisburg, Pennsylvania, vols. I–XXX.

Coulter, E. Merton. *The Confederate States of America, 1861–65.* Baton Rouge, 1950.

Davis, Burke. *Our Incredible Civil War.* New York, 1960.

Davis, William C. *The Imperiled Union.* Garden City, 1982–83.

——————, ed. *The Image of War.* 6 vols. Garden City, 1981–84.

Dupuy, R. Ernest. *Men of West Point: The First 150 Years of the U.S. Military Academy.* New York, 1951.

Faust, Patricia L., ed. *Historical Times Illustrated Encyclopedia of the Civil War.* New York, 1986.

Foote, Shelby. *The Civil War: A Narrative.* 3 vols. New York, 1958–74.

Freeman, Douglas Southall. *Lee's Lieutenants.* 3 vols. New York, 1942–44.

——————. *R. E. Lee.* 4 vols. New York, 1934-35.

Gerteis, Louis S. *From Contraband to Freedman*. Westport, Connecticut, 1973.

Hattaway, Herman and Archer Jones. *How the North Won*. Urbana, 1983.

Johnson, Rossiter. *Campfires and Battlefields*. New York, 1967.

Jones, Virgil C. *The Civil War at Sea*. 3 vols. New York, 1960–62.

Kechum, Robert M., ed. *The American Heritage Picture History of the Civil War*. Garden City, 1960.

Leech, Margaret. *Reveille in Washington*. New York, 1941.

Leckie, Robert. *None Died in Vain*. New York, 1990.

Livermore, Thomas L. *Numbers and Losses in the Civil War in America*. Boston, 1901.

Long, E. B. *The Civil War Day by Day: An Almanac*. Garden City, 1971.

Lossing, Benjamin J. *Pictorial History of the Civil War in the United States of America*. Hartford, n.d.

McPherson, James M. *Battle Cry of Freedom*. New York, 1988.

Miller, Francis T., ed. *The Photographic History of the Civil War*. 10 vols. New York, 1911.

Moehring, Eugene P. and Arleen Keylinb, eds. *The Civil War Extra from the Pages of the Charleston Mercury and the New York Times*. New York, 1975.

Nevins, Allan. *Ordeal of the Union*. 2 vols. New York, 1947.

——————. *The War for the Union*. 4 vols. New York, 1957–71.

*Official Records of the Union and Confederate Navies in the War of the Rebellion*. 39 vols. Washington, 1892–1922.

Quarles, Benjamin. *The Negro in the Civil War*. Boston, 1953.

Randall, James G. *Lincoln the President*. 4 vols. New York, 1945–55.

Roller, David C. and Robert W. Twyman, eds. *The Encyclopedia of Southern History*. Baton Rouge, 1979.

Schwab, John C. *The Confederate States*. New York, 1901.

Scott, H. L. *Military Dictionary*. New York, 1861.

Sifakis, Stewart. *Who Was Who in the Confederacy*. New York, 1988.

——————. *Who Was Who in the Union*. New York, 1988.

Smith, Page. *Trial by Fire*. New York, 1982.

Tatum, George Lee. *Disloyalty in the Confederacy*. New York, 1972.

Turner, George E. *Victory Rode the Rails*. Indianapolis, 1953.

*The War of the Rebellion: A Compilation of the Official Records of the Union and Confederate Armies*. 128 vols. Washington, 1880–1901.

Warner, Ezra J. *Generals in Blue*. Baton Rouge, 1964.

——————. *Generals in Gray*. Baton Rouge, 1959.

Welles, Gideon. *Diary of Gideon Welles*. 3 vols. New York, 1960.

Wiley, Bell I. *The Life of Billy Yank*. Indianapolis, 1952.

————. *The Life of Johnny Reb*. Indianapolis, 1943.
Williams, T. Harry. *Americans at War*. Baton Rouge, 1960.
————. *Lincoln and His Generals*. New York, 1952.
————. *Lincoln and the Radicals*. Madison, Wisconsin, 1965.
Winchester, Kenneth, ed. *Brother Against Brother*. New York, 1990.
Wagman, John, ed. *Civil War Front Pages*. New York, 1989.
Ward, Geoffrey C., et al. *The Civil War: An Illustrated History*. New York, 1990.
Yearns, Wilfred B. *The Confederate Congress*. Athens, Georgia, 1960.

# Index

*Webb Garrison is a veteran writer who lives in Lake Junaluska, North Carolina. Formerly associate dean of Emory University and president of McKendree College, he has written forty books, including* A Treasury of Civil War Tales, A Treasury of White House Tales, *and* A Treasury of Christmas Stories.